Governor Sidney J. Catts:
Florida's Bigoted Reformer

By CL Gammon

DEEP READ PRESS

Lafayette, Tennessee

www.deepreadpress.com

Copyright © 2021 by CL Gammon

All Rights Reserved. No part of this book may be reproduced, stored in a retrieval system, or transmitted in any form or by any means without permission of the publisher, except by a reviewer who may quote brief passages in a review to be printed in a newspaper, magazine, or journal.

ISBN: 978-1-954989-00-9
Cover Design by: Kim Gammon
Edited by: Kim Gammon
Published by:
DEEP READ PRESS
LAFAYETTE, TENNESSEE
www.deepreadpress.com

Governor Sidney J. Catts

The cover image is in the public domain

Governor Sidney J. Catts

For my Kimmie

Acknowledgments

I would like to thank Kim Gammon for all the hard work she did on this book.

Table of Contents

Introduction – 8
1. His Childhood – 11
2. His Education – 13
3. Preacher Catts – 15
4. Catts for Congress - 20
5. Catts for Governor - 26
6. His Supporters – 28
7. His Campaign – 30
8. The Sturkie Resolutions – 35
9. Catts and Demagoguery – 40
10. Knott Mocks Catts – 47
11. Primary Results – 49
12. Knott Nominated – 51
13. Catts Continues the Fight – 53
14. Catts and Prohibition – 60
15. Knott Fights Back – 67
16. The Newspaper War – 69
17. Election Day – 71
18. The Election Aftermath – 74
19. Catts Remains a Democrat – 76
20. Taking Office – 79
21. The Bigot Governor – 83
22. The Spoils System – 87
23. Catts and the Legislature – 97
24. The End of Cattsism – 108
25. No More Victories – 131
26. Later Life – 135
Conclusion – 136

Appendix I: Inaugural Address of Sidney J. Catts – 138

Appendix II: 1916 Prohibition Party National Platform – 151

Appendix III: Florida Election Returns from 1916 – 162

Selected Sources – 163

About the Author – 167

Index – 168

Introduction

SOME people are bigger than life – they just are. Sidney Johnston Catts, Florida's 22nd Governor was one of those people.

Florida, as was the rest of America, was in turmoil for decades after the end of the Civil War. Racism, anti-foreignism, and anti-Catholicism were rampant. The states of the old Confederacy were even more receptive to intolerance than the rest of the country. This led to the rise of several loud and rambunctious demagogues.

These demagogic hate mongers included, at different times: James E. Ferguson of Texas (1871-1944), Huey Long of Louisiana (1893-1935), James K. Vardaman (1861-1930), Theodore Bilbo (1877-1947) of Mississippi, J. Thomas Heflin of Alabama (1869-1951), Thomas Watson of Georgia (1856-1922), Cole Blease (1868-1942), "Cotton" Ed Smith (1864-1944), Benjamin Tillman (1847-1918) of South Carolina, and many others.

These men, mostly populists, broke the hold the traditional southern conservatives had held on the southern politics for years. The populists won elections across the South with wild, emotional appeals to religious and racial bigotry. If the mass of voters did not agree with the intolerance preached by these men, enough did agree to elect them to afford them great power. Despite their demagoguery and bigotry, once in office, most of these leaders initiated progressive social and economic reforms. The reforms they rammed through included the abolition of the convict lease system, restriction of child labor, improvement of working conditions in the factories and on the farms, woman suffrage, reduction of taxes on ordinary citizens and the increase of taxes on corporations, railroad regulation, increased spending on public education, prohibition and other populist legislation.

Florida's most important addition to the Southern demagoguery was one Sidney J. Catts. Catts enjoyed a meteoric rise in Florida beginning in 1916 and while he only won one election, he remained an important political figure in Sunshine State until around 1930.

While many condemned Catts, and often for good reason, one cannot doubt he made some important and positive changes in the Sunshine State during his single term as Governor.

Catts was a natural born earth shaker. He also threw convention to the wind. After the Florida Democratic Party connived with the State Supreme Court and denied him the Democratic nomination for Governor that he rightly won, he accepted the nomination of the Prohibition Party, defied all odds, and won the General Election.

This brief volume sketches the life and political career of Sidney Catts. It is a fair accounting of Catts the man and Catts the politician. There is no doubt that Sydney Catts was a great reformer and there is no doubt that he was a raging bigot. It would not be fair to the reader, or to Catts, to leave out either side of his story.

This book also looks at the age in which Catts lived and the attitudes of that age.

There is also no doubt, that Catts was a product of his environment and had he trod the earth at any other time, he could not have enjoyed the popular success he won.

In 1917, Catt became the first Governor of Florida since 1877 (during the period of Reconstruction) to represent a party other than the Democratic Party. As of this date, Catts remains the only person ever elected to a statewide office on the Prohibition ticket.

1. His Childhood

SIDNEY Johnston Catts was born near Pleasant Hill, Dallas County, Alabama on July 31, 1863. The Civil War was still raging and it was a dark time for the South. Less than a month before Catts was born, the Rebels lost the major battles of Vicksburg and Gettysburg. While the war would continue for almost two more years, the fate of the Confederacy was all but sealed. However, his father made his allegiance clear when he named his son after Confederate General Sidney Johnston.

Even though he was born during the Civil War, Catts did not suffer the hard life that many in the South did during the long Reconstruction period that followed. In fact, he grew up in a household of means.

His parents were Captain Samuel W. Catts and Adeline R. Smiley Catts. His mother's family came from Ireland and settled in the Edgefield district, South Carolina, before the Revolutionary War. His mother's grandfather commanded a portion of the South Carolina militia during the Revolution.

Catts was a direct descendant on his father's side of the famous Dutch poet and politician Jacob Catts (1577-1660). Jacob Catts was violently anti-Catholic even for a Protestant of his time. It is possible that the knowledge of his famous ancestor's hatred for Roman Catholics colored the opinions Catts held. Of course, most of the people Catts knew during his youth were anti-Catholic to the core and he did not need to look to an ancestor for an anti-Catholic role model.

Samuel Catts was a successful planter and merchant and became very wealthy. Even after the Civil War, the elder Catts retained his lands and his wealth. Samuel Catts, as was the case with almost all of his neighbors, was an unabashed Democrat. Thus, Sidney Catts grew up to be a Democrat too.

2. His Education

*B*ECAUSE of his elevated station in life, Sidney Catts was favored with opportunities that most Southern youth of his time did not enjoy. Catts was an intelligent lad, but he was something of a daydreamer and displayed indifference toward the rigors of schoolwork. However, Sidney's parents refused to allow him to go through life uneducated. They demanded his son attend good schools and get a quality education.

Blessed with the means to study anywhere he desired, Catts flew around schools like a moth about open flames. After completing his elementary education at the best private schools in Dallas County, Catts enrolled at Auburn College (now Auburn University), where he studied agriculture for three years. However, he left Auburn without a degree.

Then, in 1878, Catts studied at Howard College in Alabama (now Samford University). Again, Catts left college without a degree.

After abandoning his studies at Howard, Catts traveled the short distance to the north to Lebanon, Tennessee and he enrolled in the town's prestigious Cumberland University Law School.

The law school (now part of Samford University), founded in 1847 at Lebanon, has, over the years, produced many important officials.

To date, Cumberland alumni have included:

One United States Secretary of State

Two United States Supreme Court justices

Eight United States Senators

Nine state Governors (including Catts)

Fifty-four members of the United States House of Representatives

Hundreds of other state and local officials

The difficulty of graduating from such an institution as Cumberland did not intimidate Catts. In fact, he enjoyed the study of law and he quickly developed the discipline necessary for succeeding in conquering the challenging course work at Cumberland. He received his L. L. B. degree in 1882. It is amazing that considering his checkered scholastic past, he obtained his law degree at the tender age of 19.

Despite gaining a law degree from perhaps the most prestigious law school in the South, Catts did not care much for the practice of the profession. He did practice in Dallas County while he managed his mother's property for three years. Yet, his heart was elsewhere.

3. Preacher Catts

WHEN his duties as caretaker of his mother's plantation concluded, Sidney Catts abandoned the practice of law. About at that time, he became a devout born-again Christian and joined the Baptist church. His passion soon turned to preaching. In 1886, at twenty-three, Catts became an ordained minister and pursued what he felt was his true calling.

Catts was unlike most ministers. He was abrupt, reserved, and displayed a violent temper. According to biographer Wayne Flynt, "Sydney Catts was a visceral man who lived by the emotion of the moment, and many a temper tantrum would be followed by many a remorseful apology."

Due to his personality, it was difficult to get to know Catts and he did not make friends easily. However, he displayed great loyalty to those few friends he did have.

The same year he became ordained in the ministry, Catts married Alice May Campbell of Montgomery, Alabama. The two wed in her hometown. Their union was fruitful and it produced eight children.

Catts was an impressive preacher. The stoutly built, one-eyed minister with flaming red hair stood six feet tall and weighed about 200 pounds. He had a deep voice that resonated from the pulpit to the very back pews of even the largest of churches. He was passionate about many things, but he was particularly vocal in his condemnation of the Roman Catholic Church and the various conspiracies he believed the Catholics were perpetrating in the United States.

Catts often delivered his personal testimony to those listening to him. He referred to this speech as his "Old Black Stump Sermon." He said the voice of the Holy Spirit awakened him one day, and that it led him into a Baptist revival meeting. As he was speaking, he would look to the ceiling and say, "I knew old Catts had gone wrong." Then, he looked directly at his congregation, and said in his time of discomfort "an angel came to comfort me" as he held tight the "old black stump." Then, Catts said he was "saved."

The "Old Black Stump Sermon" was more than just a recounting of the salvation of Sidney J. Catts. It carried a secular message as well. The sermon comforted poor whites who had suffered first the Reconstruction, and then the depression of the 1890s. It also helped condition them to the idea that they were victims of minorities and Roman Catholics.

Between 1886 and 1890, Catts served as pastor of a number of churches in Dallas and Lowndes counties, Alabama. These included churches at Sandy Ridge, and Mt. Willing. Not only was he a powerful speaker, but his legal experience did him great service in his administrative duties with his churches.

After a few years ministering in and around Dallas County, Catts needed a change. He moved the 32 miles southeast from Pleasant Hill to Fort Deposit, Alabama, and was pastor of Bethel Baptist church there for five years. Then, Catts moved about 70 miles northeast from Fort Deposit to Tuskegee, Alabama. In Tuskegee, Catts led the First Baptist church for five years. At the same time, even though he had no previous military experience, Catts served as captain of the local militia unit called the Macon Guards.

After leaving the church at Tuskegee, Catts returned to his former church in Fort Deposit and ministered for another five years. In 1904, Catts engaged in a dispute with the congregation of the Bethel Baptist church. He became upset when the Deacons did not grant him as much money for missions as he wanted.

The story goes that during an emotional sermon to his Fort Deposit congregation on a hot, humid, Alabama day, Catts asked the members for a substantial mission offering. Those that attended his church were mostly poor dirt farmers who had little extra money and not one of them uttered a sound or reach for a wallet.

Catts, dripping with sweat, waited for a moment or two, then his face grew crimson, and after he had taken his handkerchief from his vest pocket and wiped away some of the perspiration. Then Catts verbally assaulted the congregation. Catts yelled at them, "I don't intend to stand here long and see you sitting like frogs waiting for it to rain. If I cannot have the support of my congregation, I shall offer my resignation!"

His words stung the congregation, but not one sound of support for Catts came from it.

Catts had become a moderately powerful force in Alabama State Baptist Convention politics. The angry minister attended the Baptist state convention in 1904, while he was still battling with his church congregation. During the convention, he spoke on "the Preacher and Politics." As will be see, Catts had already moved into the political arena.

Unable to come to an understanding with his congregation, Catts soon kept his word and resigned from the ministry of Bethel Baptist.

After leaving Bethel Baptist, Catts went back to farming, but he continued to preach from time to time, mostly in rural churches with small congregations.

Farming did not suit Catts and he was soon looking for another change. In 1911, he received an offer to be the pastor of the Baptist church at DeFuniak Springs, Florida. It was a life-changing offer for Catts. The Catts offer also proved important to the history of Florida.

Situated a few miles south of the Alabama line in the center of the Florida panhandle, between Tallahassee (about 110 miles away) to the east and Pensacola (about 80 miles away) to the west, DeFuniak Springs was an ideal spot of migration for Catts. Not only did the town have a reasonable climate, its residents had long-since embraced the beliefs, religious and political, that Catts espoused.

Energized by the sense of a new adventure, Catts packed up his family and took off for the Sunshine State.

Catts ministered to the church at DeFuniak Springs for three years and then he gave it up. He felt he needed more income than the church could provide, so he traded the pulpit for a more stable salary. He took a job as the Florida State Agent for a fraternal life insurance company.

Thus, while he still preached ocassionlly, his days as a full-time professional preacher had passed.

4. Catts for Congress

𝓑Y the time Catts left the Bethel Baptist church, his mind had already turned to politics. He felt he possessed all the qualifications to hold high office. This is no surprise. Catts had a robust ego and he believed he was the superior of most, if not all, men.

Catts was ready to serve, but he decided to bide his time until the right office became available to him. It did not take long for Catts to convince himself that his opportunity was at hand.

Charles Winston Thompson of Tuskegee, Alabama won election to Congress from Alabama's Fifth District in 1900 and he served until his death on March 20, 1904. Alabama's Governor, William Jelks, ordered that a special election to fill Thompson's seat be held at once.

Catts believed this was his opportunity to jump in the political pond and he announced his intention to seek the Democratic nomination for the seat. Catts understood that the voters of the Fifth District would certainly elect the Democratic nominee and running without the Democratic nomination was a waste of time.

Like many aspiring politicians, Catts was naïve. He assumed that his beliefs were so astute and undeniably correct, that voters would sweep him to power easily. Also like many aspiring politicians, he was in for a rude awakening.

Catts believed he could count upon the poor white voters in his district and he thought he was certain of winning the election. However, he did not consider the views of Alabama's Democratic establishment, or the power the establishment kingmakers possessed. The Democratic establishment promoted James Thomas Heflin (called Tom) for the seat. Heflin was entrenched in the Democratic Party hierarchy. Heflin had served as Mayor of Lafayette, Alabama (1893-1894), a member of the Alabama State House of Representatives (1896-1900), and as Alabama Secretary of State (1902-1904).

Catts expressed little concern regarding Heflin's outstanding qualifications, or powerful supporters. The Alabama preacher thought he could overcome any obstacle due to his pervasive skill as an orator. Catts looked to another great orator, William Jennings Bryan, for inspiration. After all, Bryan had wrestled the national Democratic Party away from the establishment easterners with little more than the power of his words. Catts reasoned that if Bryan could win over the national party, *he* should be able to win over Alabama's Fifth District.

Although he was a political novice, Catts did have some solid connections. He was by nature a joiner. Some of the organizations that counted him a member included the Free Masons, the Woodmen of the World, the Junior Order of American Mechanics, the

Knights of Pythias, and the Guardians of Liberty. Catts also belonged to a bevy of farmers' organizations. Although he was not a member of any labor union, Catts displayed sympathy for, and a little support from, labor unions of every sort. While these connections opened some doors, they offered Catts few votes.

Catts threw himself into the campaign with all the fire and brimstone one would expect from a Bible thumping Baptist. He had given a great deal of thought to what he would tell voters, and he came out of the gates in full gallop.

Beyond stressing the fact that he was a "good Christian" and that he was a long-time preacher, Catts played up his legal degree. He did this even though he had not practiced law in years, and he had never been a full-time attorney.

Catts also pulled at the heartstrings of voters. During every campaign stop, Catts went out of his way to interject mentions of his children into his speeches. He often said that children were the greatest riches in the world, and "we have a fine mess of them." While one could write off his loving words about his children as mere campaign rhetoric, there is no doubt that Catts had a genuine fondness for his kids.

Catts proclaimed his support of National Prohibition. He had spent his religious career condemning "Demon Rum" and it was only logical for him to make Prohibition an important facet of his campaign. He promised the people of his district that he would drive the backwoods bootleggers out of his district and help make Prohibition a national reality.

However, Catts soon learned that voters would not send him to Washington based upon his connections, his time behind a pulpit, his legal experience, his love of his family, or his opposition to drink alcohol. He needed red meat to excite the voters. Catts believed he had plenty of red meat to feed the voters.

Sidney Catts took the low road of demagoguery and bigotry. He first went after Roman Catholics. He was almost gleeful in enunciating his reasons for wanting to persecute Catholics. He said that during prayer, he had been "struck with awful force by the cruelties of the Roman Catholic Church towards others when in her power." He continued that history proved that God wanted to humble the Roman Catholics. He pointed out that the Protestants in England had destroyed the Grand Armada of Catholic Spain; that the Russians had had defeated Napoleon and the French Catholics; "while in the new world every movement of Jehovah seems to be directed against the temporal power of the Pope, and for enlightenment and good government."

Catts even tied his anti-Catholic message to his support of Prohibition. He battered audiences with the idea that "Romanism and Rum" were interconnected. He claimed that the Roman Catholic Church was a major proponent of the American liquor trade. Catts received loud applause whenever he attacked Catholics.

One might wonder why the voters of Alabama were receptive to the anti-Catholic message Catts delivered. In the early part of the Twentieth Century, anti-Catholic sentiment boomed throughout the United States, especially in the South. As militarism and the possibly of a world war grew in Europe, American demagogues framed the potential conflict in Europe as a battle between Protestant England and Catholic Germany. While the characterization of the problems in Europe as a Catholic against Protestant contest was utterly wrong, a large number of voters bought into the idea.

Catts did not confine his prejudice to Roman Catholics. He was also rabidly racist. For instance, he often spoke of the time when two Boston pastors spoke at Tuskegee Institute and advocated integrated schools. In reaction to the Massachusetts clergymen, an angry Catts told his audiences, mostly poor whites, that he proposed to "change his commentaries into works on military tactics – his pen and plow into a sword and . . . go down to Dallas and Lowndes (counties) and organize the boys for war."

Catts also related how in the 1890s, racial tensions ran high in Alabama. He then told the true story of how during that time, a Black man threatened him with a knife. Catts, his one good eye flashing with the fires of a hellish hatred, went into detail as to how he reacted. He told his mesmerized audiences that he raised his shotgun, and with a single blast, killed the man. Catts continued that the Sheriff arrested him, but he pled "not guilty" and claimed self-defense. He spoke proudly that an all-White jury had acquitted him. Catts implied that a no self-respecting White man would ever vote to convict another White man for killing a Black man. His audiences invariably agreed with him.

Catts had a powerful, and, sadly, an effective message. He may well have won the election, had he faced a more moderate opponent. However, Tom Heflin was also a notorious race baiter. The establishment candidate's message was just as odious and toxic as that of Catts. In fact, Heflin was often even more violent in his verbal attacks on minorities than was Catts.

On Election Day, Heflin far outpolled his opponent in the Democratic primary. Catts was gracious in defeat, but he was in no way discouraged. He still believed that in the right situation, at the right time, he could carry a congressional district, or even a state.

The politics bug had bitten Catts and he was certain that he would seek office again. However, he promised himself that he would be smarter the next time around. He had failed to link Heflin to the rich farmers and entrepreneurs in his district. He determined that the next time he sought a political office he would make his opponent into an issue. He would charge his opponent with being the tool of the rich, of minorities, and of the Catholics. He would bury his opponent with such attacks so deeply that that the man could never dig out from under them.

5. Catts for Governor

THE Florida race for Governor in 1916 was, by any estimation, extraordinary – even bizarre. The Democratic primary matched up an entrenched member of the establishment (called the "courthouse ring") against an unknown preacher turned insurance agent who had been living in the Sunshine State for only a few years. The "conventional wisdom" was that the establishment Democrat would easily dispatch the outsider and cruise to election that fall. However, there was a big surprise in store for those attempting to apply conventional wisdom.

Sidney Catts had been living in the Sunshine State only three years when, in 1914, he decided to run for the governorship of his adopted state. His travels around Florida selling insurance and preaching convinced him that the voters of "America's Playground" agreed with him on most issues. In fact, he convinced himself that if he packaged his beliefs correctly and kept up a drumbeat of attacks against those he viewed as his opponents, he could not lose.

Another point that made Catts confident of victory was the fact that in Florida, the Governors could only serve a single four-year term. Thus, Governor Park Trammell could not seek reelection. Catts thought that with Trammel barred from running for reelection, victory against another candidate was more than just possible, it was likely.

While those few who paid any attention of his plans to run at all wrote it off to an audacious and foolhardy rush into oblivion, Catts was serious in his attempt to gain the Democratic nomination for Governor. Instead of waiting to the beginning of the election year, as was the tradition, he hit the campaign trail well ahead of anyone else. Catts expected his early organizing and lonely work to pay dividends. When he made his candidacy official in early 1915, Catts had already been on the campaign trail for a year and he was convinced that his assumption was correct.

While a newcomer to America's Playground, Catts understood the political situation in his adopted state very well. He realized that Florida was a one-party state and he knew that if he prevailed in the primary and gained the Democratic nomination, dispatching the Republican nominee would be a simple task.

Catts also understood that he faced as tough a task against favorite William V. Knott as David had faced in Goliath, but, like David, he had supreme confidence. He believed that Knott would be as complacent as Goliath had been and that this giant would fall too.

6. His Supporters

CATTS identified his most likely supporters and went after them with all the enthusiasm that a born-again, Bible thumping, "Fire and Brimstone" preacher could muster. He targeted what he called the "Cracker vote." These voters (some would call them "Rednecks" today) were poorer, less educated, more rural, and more religious than most other Floridians. Most of the Crackers lived on small farms from which they scratched out a meager existence, or fished for a meager portion in the Gulf of Mexico. Beyond the hardscrabble farmers and one-boat fishermen, Catts appealed to others who earned a tiny wage doing backbreaking work for well-to-do owners of sawmills, and other businesses.

The Crackers were concentrated mostly in the Florida panhandle and in the western part of the state along the Gulf coast. One successful slogan of the Catts campaign was "Florida Crackers have only three friends in this world: God Almighty, Sears Roebuck, and Sidney Johnston Catts."

While his opponents claimed the colorful and bombastic Catts practiced gimmickry, even quackery, he didn't mind. He understood his constituency. He played on their fear, and bigotry, and the darker portion of their patriotism – their nativism. Catts often said, "Nothing in Florida above the nation's flag; the red school house against the Parochial school;

all closed institutions in Florida to be opened by process of law and America for Americans first, last and forever!"

7. His Campaign

WHILE Catts was certain that he was of the timber to be a great political leader, when he announced his intent to attempt to win the governorship, few in Florida took any notice of it and those few that did treated as a joke. This did not dissuade Catts. He knew that Florida's Democratic courthouse ring and the Sunshine State's major newspapers would always favor State Comptroller William V. Knott over him. Florida's political pundits listed Ion Farris, a progressive from Jackson who had served in both the State Legislature and the State Senate, as the chief challenger to Knott. Florida's newspapers mostly ignored Catts and the other candidates for the Democratic nomination.

William Valentine Knott lived in Leesburg, Florida. He was popular and he fit perfectly the ideal of what the establishment Democrats wanted in a Governor. In addition, he was as loyal to the leaders of Florida's courthouse ring as a politician could be. His friends told audiences that Knott displayed a higher degree of honesty and integrity than any other public man in Florida. While few believed that, it still felt good to vote for a man of such myth.

Years later, an admirer who was willing to overlook Knott's shortcomings wrote "no name has been more closely associated with real and vital service to the state at large than that of Knott."

Knott was born near the town of Dawson, Georgia on November 24, 1863. He was the son of an Indian fighter and county judge who became a plantation owner. Like Catts, Knott lived a privileged life as a youth.

Knott relocated to Leesburg in 1881 and operated an orange grove for a short time. Desiring a better paying, less physical career, went into politics. He first became the Sumterville Circuit Court Clerk. Then, in 1897, Governor William D. Bloxham took notice of Knott and appointed him State Auditor. In 1903, Governor William S. Bryan appointed Knott State Treasurer, and then in 1912, Governor Albert W. Gilchrist appointed Knott State Comptroller.

Knott also served as a member of the Board of Internal Improvement Fund, a collector for the Internal Revenue Service in Florida and finally superintendent of the Florida State Hospital at Chattahoochee.

Knott was a prohibitive favorite to win the election and become Florida's next Governor. The only real question in the minds of most was how big his landslide victory would be. Knott received endorsements from: (1) the majority of Florida's newspapers, (2) most of the state's business leaders, (3) most local political leaders, and (4) virtually all of Florida's important political leaders, including United States Senator Duncan Upshaw Fletcher and Governor Park Trammell.

Even though Knott appeared unbeatable, others besides Catts thought they could win the Democratic primary, and then the election.

Below is a list of the other somewhat important candidates:

Miami attorney Frederick M. Hudson entered the race with high hopes. A few thought that due to his connections in South Florida Hudson might just upset Knott.

The aforementioned Ion Farris of Jacksonville attempted to make a strong run. Farris had served in and held leadership roles in both houses of the Florida legislature. He had served as the Speaker or the Florida House and President of the State Senate. Farris had the backing of organized labor and the progressive wing of the Democratic Party.

Another contender was Frank A. Wood. Wood was a successful banker in St. Petersburg. He had also served in the state legislature. Because of his wealth, Wood had enough money to finance a strong campaign.

Of course, Sidney J. Catts, who had already been campaigning for almost two years, was in the race even if the media outlets in Florida did not recognize it.

Knott listened to the "experts" and became certain he would receive the nomination and would win in November. Thus, he didn't make campaigning a priority. He said that his duties as State Comptroller kept him off the campaign trail. Knott did issue a platform calling for: (1) economy in government, (2) equalization of tax laws, (3) larger pensions for Civil War veterans, and (4) improved roads.

The uninspired and insipid platform Knott presented simply aided Catts. The Baptist minister used the boredom and complacency surrounding Knott to his own advantage.

Beyond his anti-Catholic campaign, Catts, (and others) charged that Knott was lax in his duties, which had caused state bank failures in Florida. Knott denied the charges, but the banks had failed, and he could not change that fact or successfully put the blame on anyone else.

Catts also charged that Knott was in the pocket of the Florida's big railroads and multi-million-dollar corporations. He claimed that if Knott became Governor, the rich would never have to pay their fair share of taxes. Knott denied this charge as well, but with little enthusiasm.

Catts also endorsed better public education, particularly vocational training. Beyond that, he told audiences that Knott, who was in Tallahassee supposedly performing his duties as Comptroller, had no interest in improving education in the Sunshine State.

Along with attacking Knott on several counts, Catts scored points with attacks on Florida State Shellfish Commissioner T. R. Hodges. The attacks stemmed from and act of the Florida legislature and its aftermath. In 1913, the legislature passed a law that taxed and regulated shellfish fishermen. Outraged, the fishermen, especially those engaged in the oyster industry, refused to comply with the regulations, and did not pay the taxes.

The frustrated legislature decided to force the fishermen to follow the law. To this end, the lawmakers appropriated $15,000 to purchase a steamer called the *Roamer* to patrol the Gulf Coast and ensure compliance of state regulations. Governor Park Trammel signed the legislation and the state purchased the *Roamer*.

A patrol ship, at first unarmed, in the Gulf of Mexico only added to the anger of the commercial anglers. The result was many, many threats on the life of Commissioner Hodges, and other threats to sink the *Roamer*. In fact, a commercial fisherman murdered a deputy attempting to enforce the law.

Horrified by the rebellion in the gulf, Hodges ordered the arming of the *Roamer* with two cannons capable of firing one-pound balls. Although the cannons were never fired, the shellfish fishermen considered the arming of the ship as an act of war against them.

The gulf coast fishermen were part of the natural constituency of Catts. Thus, it is understandable that he would defend them and he did. Campaigning in gulf coast towns that depended upon the fishing industry for their livelihood, Catts attacked Hodges with all the power he could summon. He said that if he had been Governor, he would have vetoed the legislature's appropriation to purchase the *Roamer*. He continued with his usual bombast that when he was Governor, there would be no gunboats harassing the honest citizens of Florida.

8. The Sturkie Resolutions

CATTS received another windfall with the adoption of the *Sturkie Resolutions* by the Florida Democratic Executive Committee on January 6, 1916. R. B. Sturkie of Pasco County presented the resolutions (actually written by John M. Barrs of Jacksonville) in an attempt to, among other things, to pull the Democratic Party back from the growing climate of religious intolerance in Florida.

Until about 1910, Florida had been the most religiously tolerant state in the South. A few Catholics had even managed to win election to high public office in the Sunshine State. However, that changed when Tomas E. Watson of Georgia began publishing virulent anti-Catholic newspapers such as *The Jeffersonian* and *Watson's Magazine*.

While his papers were racist and anti-Semitic as well as being anti-Catholic, it was "exposes" on the "Roman Catholic hierarchy" in 1909 that grabbed the attention of Floridians. Watson's diatribes ignited a fire of bigotry in Florida and caused the spawning of several secret societies in the state. Organizations such as the Patriotic Sons of America and the Guardians of Liberty gained notoriety throughout the state. The secret organizations were dangerous to persons they targeted as enemies.

Two highly controversial clauses of the *Sturkie Resolutions* attempted to address and thwart the anti-Catholic movement. One clause pledged Democratic voters not to be influenced "by any religious test or on account of religious belief, denomination or sect with which the candidate is affiliated." The other controversial clause pledged that Democratic voters would not belong to "any secret organization which attempts in any way to influence political action or results."

While the purpose of the *Sturkie Resolutions* was well meaning – to break the power of secret nativist societies by keeping them out of the Democratic primaries and curbing the growing anti-Roman Catholic bias in Florida – they only added fuel those very groups they attempted to squash.

The Executive Committee adopted the *Sturkie Resolutions* by a nearly unanimous vote. Only one member of the committee dissented. While Catts was still largely unknown in the Sunshine State and Sturkie did not direct the resolutions against him specifically, Catts reacted as if Sturkie and the Florida Democratic Party had targeted him and his supporters. From January 6 onward, Catts roared that the *Sturkie Resolutions* were an example of the vast conspiracy the Florida Democratic establishment and the Catholic Church had launched against him.

More importantly, at first anyway, Democratic voters across the state reacted badly to the *Sturkie Resolutions*. Loud public rallies sprang up across the state. During these protests, thousands of ordinary Democrats signed strongly worded petitions attacking the

Sturkie Resolutions. Opponents of the resolutions dumped the petitions at the doorstep of the State Democratic Executive Committee.

There were also revolts among several local Democratic organizations. County Executive Committees in Hillsborough, Brevard, Gadsden, and other counties demanded the State Executive Committee rescind the *Sturkie Resolutions.* In addition, the politically important Florida State Federation of Labor, meeting in Tampa on February 2, 1916, demanded that the State Executive Committee reconvene and repeal the *Sturkie Resolutions.*

Of course, groups and persons across the state quickly took sides regarding *Sturkie Resolutions.* Conservative former Governor Albert W. Gilchrist and progressive incumbent Governor Park Trammell both condemned the resolutions on the shaky grounds that they discriminated against certain candidates and favored others. At least two-thirds of Florida's major newspapers sided with Sturkie and the State Executive Committee. It was the opinion of the pro-Sturkie newspapers that if the Executive Committee reversed itself, religion would become the chief issue in the race for Florida Governor.

During the height of the debate over the *Sturkie Resolutions* frontrunner Knott made the worse mistake of his political career. In an attempt to solidify his support among the establishment Democrats and the newspapers they controlled, Knott gave his unqualified support to the Executive Committee and to the

Sturkie Resolutions. This blunder most likely cost Knott the election.

Despite the support the *Sturkie Resolutions* received, the Executive Committee finally gave in to the intense pressure by its opponents and in late February, State Democratic Party Chair, George P. Raney of Tampa, called the Executive Committee back into session in order to reconsider the *Sturkie Resolutions*.

The Executive Committee had one of its most contentious meetings ever. Finally, after many long arguments and red faces, the Executive Committee voted 26 to 14 to repeal the *Sturkie Resolutions*. Those supporting the *Sturkie Resolutions* saw dark times ahead. In a Page 1 editorial, the Jacksonville *Florida Times-Union* made dire predictions. The writer predicted that Floridians could "now look for the nastiest, most abusive campaign that Florida has ever known, and it will probably be attended with loss of life."

Later, many analysts concluded that Catts won the election because of the *Sturkie Resolutions* and the controversy he stirred up because of them. While that may be an overstatement, the dispute over the resolutions certainly split the courthouse ring and aided Catts.

While there is no hard evidence that the Executive Committee was targeting Catts with the *Sturkie Resolutions*, he certainly played it as if he were the victim of the committee. He condemned the committee as a tool of the Roman Catholics and, with the help of fundamentalist preachers such as Reverend

Billy Parker spread his message across the state.

9. Catts and Demagoguery

SIDNEY Catts was not above spreading fear to gain votes. He doled out all kinds of conspiracy theories in his attempt to endear himself to the voters of Florida.

Catts told his supporters that Democratic Party leaders in Florida were Pharisees. He said to them, "Nothing in Florida above the nation's flag: the red schoolhouse against the parochial school. America for Americans, first, last and forever!"

In addition, he spread other ridiculous conspiracy theories concerning the Catholics and the Pope. Catts was so successful that he even convinced a good number of moderate Protestants to join his campaign. Writing about the campaign many years later, future Governor of Florida, Fuller Warren stated that Catts "hanged the Pope to every oak tree in West Florida." Catts was bold in his assertion that he had caused the downfall of the *Sturkie Resolutions*.

Catts and his agents related many fanciful and sensational stories regarding the alleged abuses of the Catholic Church. Some of the stories were old and had been around for decades, while a few were the invention of Catts and those associated with him. Catts and his cohorts claimed that the Pope Benedict XV had ordered the Roman Catholics to engage in an armed revolt designed to overthrow the United States and name the pontiff, King of the

United States. Catts claimed that the Catholic revolutionaries were storing arms in the basement of the cathedral at Tampa in West Florida. That there was no cathedral in Tampa was a fact that Catts and his fellow bigots did not know, or if they did, they didn't mention it.

Later, Catts claimed that the monks residing at St. Leo's Abbey in St. Leo (near Tampa) intended to organize Florida's African American population to aid them in overthrowing Florida and establishing a foothold in North America for Germany's monarch, Kaiser Wilhelm II. He added to that absurdity by saying that if Germany won World War I, Pope Benedict XV would transfer the Holy See to San Antonio, Florida.

Catts also had dire warnings for Protestants if the Catholic revolution in the United States succeeded. He sent shivers through his audiences when he told them that the new Catholic dictatorship would torture and otherwise persecute all Protestants under its rule.

Catts blamed the Democratic establishment, both state and national, for allowing the Catholics to gain so much power in the United States and his beloved Florida. He lambasted President Woodrow Wilson for appointing a Catholic to be his secretary. Oddly, most observers at that time considered Wilson very anti-Catholic.

Catts and his associates flew to the defense of organizations that also spread the anti-Catholic message. One of them was the violently anti-Catholic Guardians of Liberty.

Founded in Washington D.C. on June 9, 1911, the Guardians of Liberty organization was never the largest anti-Catholic organization in the United States, but the important military leaders who acted as its leaders make it noteworthy. A couple of the officers of the Guardians of Liberty included Lieutenant General Nelson Miles and Rear Admiral G. W. Bard.

The religious issue caused a great deal of unnecessary consternation in Florida. An article in the *Gainesville Sun* lamented the situation thusly, "Never in the history of Florida has politics been worse mixed than at the present time. Personal friends hold aloof from discussing political candidates in many instances simply because religious prejudice has entered into the fitness of men for office and feeling is so tense that they realize it is useless to discuss the merits of candidates."

It is interesting that Catts could gain as much traction as he did, considering that there were so few Catholics in Florida at that time. Counting men, women, and children, there were fewer than 40,000 Catholics in all of Florida in 1916.

Most of Florida's hundreds of newspapers attacked the flourishing anti-Catholic bigotry in the state. However, the ordinary "Florida Cracker" had long-since been caught up in the extremism Catts and his ilk preached. Every time a newspaper attacked any anti-Catholic politician or organization, it made the anti-Catholic movement stronger. In addition, the newspaper attacks on the bigots increased the strength of Catts. Catts answered the attacks on him and his supporters by claiming that the newspapers were mere tools of the Catholics.

No matter what else one may say about Sidney J. Catts, one cannot deny that he could whip up a crowd. He was colorful and his message was as entertaining as it was toxic. Additionally, Catts was ahead of his time in some ways. For instance, he increased the scope of his campaign by traveling to towns where other candidates never visited.

Catts appeared to be everywhere at once and to some in the small towns in western Florida, Catts seemed to be the only candidate in the race. This was especially true since Knott chose to spend most of the campaign in Tallahassee allegedly taking care of his official duties.

Catts was a true innovator. While the other candidates only spoke in towns easily reached by train, Catts drove his Model T Ford to places off the beaten path. No candidate for Governor had ever honored these towns with a visit before and it made a major impact upon them. Catts also made use of loudspeakers when he was addressing large crowds. Thus, his bold, booming voice rang throughout rural Florida, both figuratively and literary.

Catts also made good use of props in his quest to win the highest office in Florida. He claimed that the Catholics had hired assassins to kill him and that he had to campaign armed. Catts said the threat from the Pope's henchmen forced him to address crowds "with both hands on my pistols, which were loaded in every chamber." He said later, "Often I would have to show them to men in the audience and tell them I would not hesitate to use them, before they would let me alone."

The voters were duly impressed by the fact that Catts was willing to risk his life to represent *their* interests. The truth is that Catts never produced any evidence that a conspiracy to murder him ever existed. The pistol-packing candidate was a great showman. His use of six shooters as campaign props drew attention to him, and he gained notoriety from his antics.

Another strong point for Catts was his unabashed support for Prohibition at both the state and national level. The Crackers, especially in the West Florida Panhandle, were infatuated with the Prohibition movement and Catts engendered their admiration with his attacks on "Demon Rum" and those who peddled it. However, the opposition to drink alcohol did not end with the Crackers. The move toward Prohibition was a national phenomenon. The Anti-Saloon League, led nationally by the likes of Purley Baker and Wayne Wheeler, was a potent opponent of the alcohol industry in the United States.

However, in Florida, the most important anti-drink organization was the Woman's Christian Temperance Union (WCTU). The WCTU, led nationally by Anna Adams Gordon and in Florida by the dynamic Minnie E. Neal, was relentless in its opposition to alcohol. County by county in the Sunshine State, the WCTU beat down the candidates of the liquor traffickers with convincing rhetoric about the dangers of alcohol abuse and whipped them consistently at the ballot box.

The anti-liquor environment created by the Anti-Salon League, the WCTU, and Protestant preachers, made Catts much more acceptable to Floridians as a whole than he otherwise may have been.

Catts was an unrelenting candidate. He travelled across the small of towns of Florida with his Bible in one hand and his revolver in the other. He would pull off his old, threadbare dress coat, roll up his sleeves, and talk to voters with the passion of a tent revival preacher. Standing in the baking sun and with sweat pouring from every pore, and implore the Crackers to save themselves by making him their next Governor. He told his audiences (who came for the show, but were soon won over by the message) that he based his political philosophy "Religion, Race, and Rum."

The large, red-faced, one-eyed, demagogue preyed on the fears of his audiences. He would take a drink of cold water dipped from a nearby bucket, wipe his brow with his large sweat-stained handkerchief, and promise his all-White audiences that he would protect them from the three things they feared most: (1) African American Equality, (2) The Catholic Church, and (3) Alcohol.

While some historians doubt that Catts actually had any real opposition to drink alcohol, or even any deep animosity toward the Catholic Church, his violent racism is not in dispute.

Strangely, the Catts agenda included several (for the time) radically progressive items. He expressed support for women's suffrage, taxation of church property, and a state income tax. His progressive agenda worried Floridians more than did his assaults on Catholics.

10. Knott Mocks Catts

THOSE supporting William V. Knott for the Democratic nomination did not take Catts seriously. When they fired back at Catts, they usually did so by trying to make him look foolish. The Knott camp attacked Catts as an ignorant opportunist. They ridiculed the preacher every chance they got. Those opposed to Catts circulated the rumor that he only became interested in running for Governor when he learned that if he won the election, he could live in the Governor's mansion rent-free.

The story the Knott campaign circulated went like this:

In 1914, Catts attended a religious conference in Tallahassee. As a part of the conference, Catts visited the Governor's Mansion and he had a conversation with Governor Park Trammell. According to the Florida Secretary of State at the time, Robert Andrew Gray, Catts asked Park, "How much rent does this place cost?"

The surprised Governor replied that the Governor stayed there free of charge.

Upon hearing that he could live in the beautiful mansion rent free, Catts became very excited and he immediately toured the entire compound including the stables and the attic. Within minutes of learning he could live in the Governor's Mansion without paying rent, he decided to seek the governorship in 1916.

Of course, Gray and Trammel were both political opponents of Catts, and the story was utterly false, but it irritated Catts. It did not cost him very many votes, however. In fact, the story illustrated the problem the Knott campaign had with Catts. Knott and his campaign managers simply did not take Catts seriously and could not believe that he was a threat. By the time the Knott campaign realized that Catts was capable of winning the nomination, it was too late to stop his momentum. All they could hope for was that the power brokers in Florida could use their political machine and bend enough arms to keep the preaching insurance man from becoming Governor of Florida.

11. Primary Results

On June 6, 1916, Florida's primary voters went to the polls after the confusing campaign. However, the primary ballot for Governor was no less confusing. Poorly thought-out election laws can cause unexpected problems. This has been the case in Florida several times and it was especially true in the Sunshine State in 1916.

The Florida legislature had desired to save the cost of runoff elections by introducing a single primary system. To accomplish this, the legislature passed the Bryan Primary Law of 1913. The new law introduced a system whereby voters cast one ballot for their favorite and another ballot for their second choice. Election officials determined the top two finishers by the first place votes they received. Then, they added the first *and* second place votes the top two finishers received and declared the person with the highest total elected.

In 1916, Florida employed the Bryan Primary Law Florida for the first time in a contest for Governor and it caused massive confusion because many voters had no idea as to what their votes actually represented. This caused long delays in voting. Election officials were confused as well and this caused even more delays in counting the ballots.

When the Canvassing Board tallied the votes from the Governor's race, (it did not finally get the votes tabulated for a full two weeks after the polls closed), they determined that Catts and Knott were the top two finishers and that Catts was the rightful nominee. The vote totals as certified by the Canvassing Board were:

Catts: 30,092 first place votes and 3,891 second place votes, totaling 33,983.

Knott: 24,765 first place votes and 8,674 second place votes, totaling 33,439.

The returns indicated clearly that Catts was the choice of Florida's Democrats. He outdistanced Knott by more than 5,000 in first place votes. However, Knott was not out of the race just yet.

Knott claimed that his loss was not legal. He held that there were "irregularities" in more than 100 of Florida's precincts and he demanded a recount. The powerful Democratic courthouse ring filed a suit with the Florida State Supreme Court asking it to order a recount. Good party men populated the Florida's High Court and they ruled that the Sunshine State must recount the vote.

12. Knott Nominated

*F*ROM the minute the recount began, Catts condemned it as a thinly veiled attempt to thwart the will of the voters and to steal the nomination for Knott. Catts became personal in his condemnation of the party insiders and William Knott, whom Catts referred to as their "puppet." Catts accused Knott partisans of committing "gigantic frauds" in altering and disallowing ballots.

Knowing he had the advantage, Knott took the high road publicly. He contended that he simply wanted the will of the voters respected. Of course, no one believed that. The people of Florida, even Knott supporters, understood that the recount was nothing more than a cynical election steal.

Surprisingly, R. B. Sturkie, whom Catts had attacked ruthlessly and denounced as a tool of the courthouse ring and the Pope, sided with Sidney Catts during the recount controversy. Sturkie stated his view that Catts had won the primary fairly and the recount was an attempt to overturn the legitimate primary results. If Catts was grateful to Sturkie, he did not make a point of saying so.

Catts, understanding that the party insiders were going to overturn the primary, promised to run in the general election in November regardless of the outcome of the recount.

The recount was at best dubious. Election officials – mostly party insiders – counted and counted again, added, and subtracted votes until the recount was complete on September 21. The new total gave the nomination to Knott by 23 votes. With the Democratic nomination finally in hand, Knott seemed on his way to the Governor's Mansion.

For his part, Catts was serious about continuing his campaign regardless of the fact that Knott was the official Democratic nominee. Again, the power brokers in Florida's Democratic Party scoffed at the one-eyed, crimson-haired preaching insurance agent. They felt that Catts would go down in inglorious defeat in November and that the bombastic outsider would disappear from Florida's political scene forever.

Once again, Florida's political elite would rue the day they underestimated the Panhandle's number one Cracker.

13. Catts Continues the Fight

*T*HE successful effort to deny Catts the Democratic nomination backfired in the end. A large number of Floridians who originally opposed Catts came to view the legal fight and the dubious recount as an election steal. These voters viewed Catts as a martyr and Knott as a criminal. In addition, and perhaps more importantly, a good number of Florida newspapers changed course and endorsed Catts.

The conspiracy to nominate Knott over him energized Catts. The crowds grew larger in the fall and as the General Election grew closer, Catts became more and more convinced that he would win. He campaigned daily, driving over the highways and dirt roads, and goat paths of Florida.

Despite what the Democratic Party leaders said, there was no doubt that a narrow plurality of Florida's voters favored Catts. As time went along, due to the urging of Catts and his friends, more and more persons saw the recount and nothing but the shabby, backroom shenanigans of a powerful political elite. As Election Day neared, Catts gained more and more momentum and Knott and his allies could do nothing to slow him down.

Catts saw his political organization blossom into a diverse collection of persons with varying views. Beyond his core supports that had been with him since the beginning, a large number of party regulars that opposed the recount came aboard his campaign.

In the primary, the political amateur Catts saw his fall campaign operated by an amalgamation of other amateurs and a smattering of professional pols. Mostly loyal political amateurs made up his primary campaign brain trust. J. V. Burke managed his campaign – to the extent that it anyone managed it at all. A close friend of Catts, DeFuniak Springs attorney, W. W. Flournoy, argued against the recount before the Florida Supreme Court. W. Bryan Mack of the *Pensacola News* acted as the campaign's liaison with other newspapers. Former Jacksonville Mayor, Van C. Swearingen, and member of the Florida Democratic Executive Committee from Tampa, Dr. W. H. Cox handled the Catts campaign in West and South Florida. Another important cog in the pre-primary season was traveling sewing machine salesman, Jerry W. Carter. Carter heard Catts speak and the one-eyed preacher enthralled him. Carter employed his considerable skills of persuasion with West Florida Crackers on the behalf of Catts.

After the primary, Catts witnessed an influx of new recruits joining his campaign. Some of these persons became very important to his effort. Former Florida State Senator J. S. Blitch of Williston had previously condemned the *Sturkie Resolutions* and he was an effective speaker for Catts across the Sunshine State.

Lake City attorney James B. Hodges was one of Florida's most savvy political operatives.

Hodges had employed his considerable skills on behalf of Knott in the primary, but he was appalled when the Knott forces stole the nomination from Catts. In August, Hodges threw his full support and provided a variety services to the flaming haired candidate. Hodges collected donations, circulated petitions, spoke for Catts in front of large crowds, and pushed back against those Democrats opposed to Catts.

The new aid was welcome, but the political experts did not decide the outcome of the election. It was Catts himself who tilted the contest. He oozed with vulgar charisma, and he was a dynamic and energetic campaigner.

Between June and November 1916, he made seven trips across Florida in his Model T. Catts had virtually no money available, thus, after each stop, he would pass the hat in an attempt to raise enough funds to fill up his car with gas before moving on to the next town. He always received enough donations to keep his caravan rolling along.

Catts was an amazing draw. He spoke to some of the largest crowds in the history of Florida politics. In some cases, the entire population of small towns and hamlets showed up at his rallies. Like a master snake charmer, the flamboyant Catts never disappointed his audiences.

In the post-primary campaign, Catts did not move away from the issues that had worked for him previously. He attacked the "Catholic menace" with the same vigor as before. In fact, he was stronger in his attacks on the Church of

Rome than previously. He told his audiences that the Catholic Church, apparently with the approval of the Pope, had funded the June recount to ensure that the Church's candidate received the nomination. He also continued to allege that a group of Catholics in Apalachicola had embarked upon a scheme to assassinate him. Because of this, said Catts, he continued to bear his two pistols. However, he had no fear of being assaulted.

By 1916, World War I had engulfed Europe for two years. Catts, like most Americans, supported the English and the French against the German "Huns" and their allies. Of course, Catts could not help but to demagogue the issue. He attacked the Germans vociferously, but he did not stop there. He accused German-Americans, of conspiring with the Catholic Church to overthrow the United States.

Catts was an unrepentant racist and was unabashed in his support of segregation. While bigoted propaganda had been around forever, the new medium of motion pictures gave much greater circulation to organized hatred. In 1915, the film *Birth of a Nation* appeared. This movie spurred the revival of the Ku Klux Klan and made voters, especially those who thought it to be an accurate and historical depiction of life, much more receptive to the demagoguery of those like Sidney J. Catts.

Another issue Catts hit hard was the lack of public morality. He said that high school girls were trying to see "how low they could cut their dresses at the top and how high they could cut them at the bottom."

Catts also stated his support for trade schools that would train students in the manual arts. He continued to condemn secondary schools that taught courses students could not apply in the real world after graduation.

Of course, Catts also played the victim to the hilt throughout the fall campaign. At every stop, he blasted the Democratic Party machine that had thwarted the will of the voters. In addition, he condemned the "Court of Supreme Contempt" which had "stolen" the Democratic nomination from him. Catts made a strong case that the powerbrokers in Florida's Democratic establishment had spit in the face of the voters and crushed Democracy into the ground with their heavy, hobnailed boots.

Catts also attacked the large corporations that he implied controlled the Democratic Party, and he called for reforms such as voting rights for women. Of course, Catts also continued to bang away at the liquor barons and promised that he would drive them out of Florida. He also promised that Prohibition would come to Florida if the voters elected him.

Specific issues notwithstanding, Catts found his greatest appeal from his identification with ordinary Floridians. He told the working class, the farmers, the small commercial fishers, the small shop owners, and everyone else who worked long hours for short pay, that he was one of them and they believed him. The phrase, "The crackers of Florida have only three friends left: God Almighty, Sears and Roebuck, and Sidney J. Catts" was repeated thousands of times in rural Florida and ordinary Floridians agreed with it.

Catts was also head and shoulders above Knott and the Republican nominee George W. Allen, when it came to personal campaigning, He put his years of experience as a preacher to use and he wowed his audiences.

Catts also employed "dirty tricks" in his campaign for Governor. Supporters of the preacher dressed as Priests, went to the most anti-Catholic areas of Florida, and campaigned *for* Knott. The fake Priests told voters they spoke for the Pope and that he was appealing for them to vote for Knott. The ruse was at least somewhat effective. There were reports of irate citizens threatening to kill the next Priest that came among them.

Another dirty trick took place on the day before the election. Catts supporters went into anti-Catholic areas and proclaimed that Knott was actually a member of the Roman Catholic faith. They offered no evidence to prove their rumors were true, but they didn't have to offer proof. The charge alone was enough to win votes for Catts.

Catts found original ways to promote his campaign. He even used a tax to his advantage. In Florida in 1916, in order to vote, a man (women could not vote) had to pay a special "Poll Tax." The Catts campaign incorporated the need to pay the Poll Tax into a catchy pro-Catts jingle: "Register Mr. Voter – Kill the Rats – Pay Your Poll Tax and VOTE for CATTS."

The United States outlawed Poll Taxes in 1964 with the ratification of the 24th Amendment.

14. Catts and Prohibition

SEVERAL anti-alcohol factions came together and formed the national Prohibition Party on September 1, 1869. From that point on, the Prohibition Party has taken an active role in both local and national politics. In the late 19th and early 20th centuries, the Prohibition Party helped elect several governors across the United States on "fusion" tickets. That is, the Prohibition Party endorsed candidates that had already won a major party nomination. However, the Prohibition Party had never elected a governor on its own. The party leadership hoped this would change when its members nominated Sidney Johnston Catts after the Democratic establishment jilted him. Catts rewarded the Prohibitionists by running roughshod over his opponents and over the Democratic Party's courthouse ring in Florida.

In late June 1916, as the Democratic Party establishment battled to rip the Democratic nomination from Catts, the Independent Prohibition Party of Florida held its state convention. Some of the most respected members of the party pushed for the nomination of Catts. The influence of these long-time Prohibition Party leaders resulted in the nomination of long-winded preacher as its candidate for Governor.

The truth was that while the Prohibition movement in Florida was strong and growing, the Prohibition Party was not. In 1912, J. W. Bingham had gained the Prohibition Party nomination for Governor and polled only 1,061 votes (2.19%). The Florida Prohibition Party leadership reasoned that they needed a strong, well-known candidate and they were willing to take a chance on the pro-Prohibition Catts.

The leadership of the Florida Prohibition Party was happy to have Catts as their nominee. Most, but not all, of the regular party membership also favored his nomination. The Prohibition Party had always been a progressive party and some members found themselves somewhat embarrassed by the extreme rhetoric Catts often spouted. The reservations of the few notwithstanding, the Florida prohibitionists universally agreed that Catts was the best candidate they had ever had.

Much to his delight, Prohibition Party National Chairman, Virgil G. Hinshaw, was witnessing the party achieve its greatest electoral successes. Hinshaw, who had chaired the party since 1904, and would remain at the helm until 1924, had seen Charles Randall of California win a seat in Congress in 1914 (Randall served until 1921) and now, he was ecstatic that the Prohibition Party had a chance of winning the governorship of a state.

Not only did the State Prohibition Party aid Catts, but the Woman's Christian Temperance Union of Florida worked hard to elect him as well. The Florida WCTU liked Catts for his opposition to alcohol, but also for his support for the political rights of women.

As stated earlier, not all the Prohibitionists supported Catts, but a brief look at the broad-based Prohibition national party platform indicates that the party had much in common with him:

(1) The platform denounced the liquor trade. It stated that liquor trafficking was "a crime – not a business" – and should have no governmental sanction.

(2) The party platform called for the ratification of a new constitutional amendment prohibiting the "manufacture, importation, exportation, transportation and sale of alcoholic beverages . . ."

(3) The platform demanded the full enfranchisement of women. The party favored amendments to the Federal and state constitutions to achieve full suffrage.

(4) The Prohibition Party committed itself to a "policy of peace and friendliness with all nations." It condemned the "wasteful military" spending in which prohibitionists claimed the Democrats and Republicans indulged.

(5) The platform made the bold statement that "Militarism protects no worthy institution. It endangers them all. It violates the high principles which have brought us as a Nation to the present hour."

(6) Prohibitionists favored the creation of a World Court that had the power to settle international disputes. The decrees of this court would have "binding force."

(7) The party called for the dismantling of the navies and disbanding of the armies of the world.

(8) The platform opposed the military draft.

(9) The prohibitionists opposed companies profiting from the manufacture of materials used for war.

(10) The platform favored utilizing the army in some ways, such as for public works projects. In addition, the party called for turning a portion of the navy into a merchant marine force.

(11) The Prohibition Party supported free trade and reciprocal trade agreements with other nations.

(12) The prohibitionists opposed President Wilson's policy of intervention in Mexico. The platform stated, "Mexico needs not a conqueror, but a good Samaritan."

(13) The Prohibition Party opposed President Wilson's policy in the Philippines.

(14) The platform favored the "conservation of forests, water power and other natural resources."

(15) Prohibitionists favored making civil service laws stronger and expanding the "merit system."

(16) The prohibitionists made a strong point of stating, "WE stand for Americanism."

(17) The party called for "uniform marriage and divorce laws, the extermination of polygamy and the complete suppression of the traffic in women and girls."

(18) The prohibitionist platform called for arbitration to settle labor disputes, an end to child labor, an eight-hour workday and at least one day a week off from work for laborers.

(19) The party promised to "foster the physical and moral well-being of the unborn."

(20) The Prohibition Party called for an extension of Employers' Liability Acts.

(21) The party pledged itself to administer the government in a business-like manner. This would, according to the prohibitionists, lead to the "abolition of useless offices, bureaus and commissions; economy in the expenditure of public funds; efficiency in governmental service; and the adoption of the budget system."

(22) The prohibitionists endorsed the concept of the line-item veto.

(23) The party called for a single, six-year term for Presidents.

(24) The Party called for "public ownership or control of all such utilities by the people and their operation and administration in the interests of all the people."

(25) The Prohibition Party called for an "absolute separation of church and state with the guaranty of full religious and civil liberty."

(26) The party called for the "equality of all before the law; in old-age pensions and insurance against unemployment and in help for needy mothers."

(27) The party also called for the adoption of laws allowing "initiative, referendum and recall."

(28) While promising the support of farming, the Prohibition Party promised the "abolition of any Board of Trade, Chamber of

Commerce, or other place of gambling in grain or trading in 'options' or 'futures' or 'short-selling,' or any other form of so-called speculation wherein products are not received or delivered, but wherein so-called contracts are settled by the payment of 'margins' or 'differences' through clearing houses or otherwise."

(29) The Prohibition Party issued strong support for "free and open markets based upon legitimate supply and demand, absolutely free from questionable practices or market manipulation."

(30) The Prohibition Party pleaded with the people not to vote along traditional party lines. The Prohibition platform stated, "The triumph of neither old political party is essential to our safety or progress. The defeat of either will be no public misfortune." Then, the party of National Prohibition charged that the Republican and Democratic parties were actually a single party. The Prohibition Platform stated that, "By age and wealth, by membership and traditions, by platforms and in the character of their candidates, they are the Conservative Party of the United States." On the other hand, the Prohibition Party claimed it was "the only great Progressive Party."

See Appendix II for the complete Prohibition Party platform of 1916.

Interestingly, while Sidney Catts supported national and state Prohibition, he was never a member of the Prohibition Party. He was in no hurry to embrace the Prohibition Party nomination and did not do so officially until October 9. The truth is that the Prohibition Party nomination did help Catts a little, but it did nothing for the Prohibition Party either nationally or in the Sunshine State.

15. Knott Fights Back

OF course, Knott and his allies did not abandon the field to Catts. The majority of Florida's newspapers endorsed Knott, even after the recount, and they redoubled their efforts to herd their readers toward him. Editors fell over themselves in lauding Knott. In addition, virtually all-important Democratic office holders accepted the recount and threw their support behind Knott. United States Senator Duncan Upshaw Fletcher and outgoing Governor Park Trammel vocally endorsed the State Comptroller.

Knott proved he was not above spreading his own conspiracy theories. He claimed that the *Sturkie Resolutions* were the result of a "frame-up" devised by Sturkie and Catts to do harm to the Knott campaign.

Knott believed that if the voters of Florida accepted him as the legitimate Democratic nominee, they would elect him easily. He charged that Catts was no Democrat and that the preacher opposed the reelection of Woodrow Wilson. Knott and his allies held that Catts supported, and would vote for the Prohibition presidential nominee, former Indiana Governor James Frank Hanly. Catts feared that too close an association with the Prohibitionists would harm him and he publicly denied any support for Hanly.

The Knott campaign continued to hammer away at Catts for being something other than a true Democrat. A person speaking for Knott in Brooksville told the audience that the Catts manager in south Florida, Dr. W. H. Cox, had never been a Democrat. The Knott supporter stated that Cox was a Populist in the 1890s, and when the Populists merged with the Democrats, Cox joined the Socialist Party. Finally, Knott's man accused Cox of supporting Theodore Roosevelt and the Progressive ("Bull Moose") Party in 1912.

Knott also accused Catts of treason against the Sunshine State. The Knott campaign spread a rumor that if Catts did not win the November election, he and his supporters intended to raise a citizens' army of 10,000 men, march on Tallahassee, overthrow the state government, and occupy the Governor's Mansion.

The rumor of generalissimo Catts and his Cracker Army overthrowing the Florida government was so ridiculous that even those most ardent in support of Knott did not believe it. The conspiracy theories spread by Knott hurt him and did nothing to damage Catts.

16. The Newspaper War

THE fall campaign drew great interest across the state and the newspapers fought it just as hard as did the candidates. Many of those papers ignored the truth while scalding their opponents.

The editors of *Tampa Tribune* changed course and supported Catts. The editors loaded their pens with venom and unloaded them while condemning the recount as a slap at democracy.

The Jacksonville *Florida Times-Union* encouraged voters to rebel against Democratic Executive Committee and split their tickets in November. Of course, the *Times-Union* was advising the citizens to vote for the Prohibition Party nominee, Sidney Catts.

The *Sanford Herald* backed Frederick Hudson in the primary. Now, the paper condemned the recount, endorsed Catts, and stated without qualm that Catts had won the Democratic primary.

Catts was pleased that his hometown paper, the *DeFuniak Breeze* defended him in the strongest terms possible. The *Breeze* implied that Knott was under the thumb of special interests: "It has been asked who is financing Mr. Catts' campaign? The great common people with voluntary contributions of from a nickel up . . . (But) who is putting up the thousands of dollars that have been expended for Mr. Knott?"

The *Lakeland Ledger* defended Catts and his Crackers by mocking Knott. The editors asked readers if they had ever seen "a more hayseed looking and acting candidate than Knott?"

Yet, the majority of the state newspapers endorsed Knott and they were relentless in their attacks upon Catts:

The *St. Petersburg Times* endorsed William Knott because he was the Democratic nominee. An editorial in the paper explained that, "The *Times* is a Democratic [Party] newspaper.... Because it is a Democratic newspaper, it believes in the doctrine of party loyalty.... Shall Florida be the first Southern state to weaken the chain of the Solid South?" In other words, the Times asked its readers to support Knott even if he had stolen the nomination.

The *Pensacola Journal* continued the tactic it employed against Catts during the primary campaign. The paper attempted to make Catts seem like a fool when an editorial claimed, "Every time Catts says anything he hits the nail on the thumb."

One thing not many Florida newspapers reported on took place on October 7, 1916. On that cool, sunny Saturday afternoon, the Georgia Tech football team steamrolled Cumberland University's squad to the tune of 222 to 0. Neither did Catts mention the debacle his alma mater suffered of the gridiron.

17. Election Day

While there were no opinion polls – at least no scientific opinion polls – taken in 1916, Catts, and his supporters, were excited on Election Day. They felt the momentum was on their side from the time the State Supreme Court allowed the dubious recount. Nothing during the summer and autumn occurred to change their minds. Catts was certain he would win the election – barring another cynical election "steal."

The Knott campaign staff expressed "hope" that somehow their champion would prevail. However, a good many of those in the Knott camp seemed to be blind to the fact that their man was in deep trouble. In fact, some of the Knott supporters expected him to win in a landslide.

Republican, George Allen had no real hopes of winning, but he felt that if Catts and Knott split the Democratic vote and he did much better than expected, perhaps, just perhaps, he could spring an upset for the ages.

Catts got another break because in Florida in those days, there was no party designation on the ballot and many voters could not tell which of the candidates the Democratic nominee was. Many voters mistakenly believed that Catts was the Democratic nominee and this helped him among those who voted strictly by party affiliation. However, this alone did not account for the outcome.

On November 7, 1916, the voters of Florida went to the polls and after the bitterest campaign in the history of the Sunshine State, officials counted the votes, and relayed that the impossible had happened. An unknown, one-eyed, red-haired, heavy-set, demagogue running on a third-party ticket had won the election and in January, he would become Governor. The Florida Crackers rejoiced. They already had their God Almighty and their Sears Roebuck, now they had their Governor Catts as well.

The vote total was:

Catts: 39,546 (47.7%)

Knott: 30,343 (36.6%)

George Allen (Republican): 10,333 (12.5%)

C. C. Allen (Socialist): 2,470 (3%)

Noel A. Mitchell (Independent): 193 (0.2%)

While he failed to receive a majority of the vote, Catts was the clear and indisputable winner. The total for Catts is all the more remarkable when one looks at the presidential results in Florida for 1916. That year, the Democratic nominee, President Woodrow Wilson, garnered more than two-thirds of the vote in the Sunshine State, while the Prohibition candidate, James Hanly finished last in a field of four, and picked up only a little more than one vote in twenty.

The Governor's race garnered such interest that the vote increased by 170% from four years earlier. Additionally, more Floridians cast votes for Governor (82,885) than voted in the Presidential race that year (80,734). It is unusual for a "down ticket" race to outpoll a Presidential contest, but 1916 was an unusual year in Florida politics in virtually every way.

18. The Election Aftermath

WHEN the election officials certified that Catts was victorious, some of his erstwhile opponents were quick to attempt to bury the hatchet with him. One opposition newspaper praised him for his "meteoric career in which he rose from private life to the state's highest office within a single year." Nationally too, Catts received kudos. The *New York Times* called his victory "spectacular."

Another newspaper marveled at the Catts victory in a long editorial published soon after the election. The writer stated, "The successful candidate was an entire stranger to the people of Florida when he announced his candidacy. His first announcements were greeted with derision – as a political joke. It is doubtful if there were more than a dozen citizens of Florida who entertained the slightest idea that he had a possible chance. Yet he defeated four of the strongest and best-known men in the State. He had against him not only these four men and their following, but practically the solid liquor influence, office-holding influence, Catholic influence, and the State press. He made the race practically without a campaign fund. Throughout the campaign, he boldly denounced from the stump certain things, which no candidate for office in Florida had ever dared to denounce, pursuing a campaign policy, which had always theretofore been considered equivalent to political suicide. Yet this man, a new comer, virtually a stranger, with no record of public performance to stand upon, with no part in the history of the State, political, commercial or otherwise, has been chosen as its governor."

19. Catts Remains a Democrat

CATTS did not intend to be an outsider for very long. He intended to rejoin the Democratic Party immediately, and to make himself its undisputed leader. The morning after the election, Catts issued a victory statement. While the membership of the Prohibition Party had worked hard for Catts, he allowed them to enjoy their first statewide electoral victory for less than a single day.

In his statement, he assured Florida's voters that he was not a "fanatic" and that he was a good Democrat who would appoint nothing but Democrats to state office in Florida. Below is the complete text of the victory statement Catts released.

TO THE PEOPLE OF FLORIDA

I appreciate the fact that Florida is the "Playground of the Americas," and I will be happy and content to continue its up building. I am a broad-minded man, and not a fanatic, as has been so often charged in this heated campaign, and will work to up build, and not tear down, what is destined to be the greatest State in the Union.

You can say for me that I will appoint every Democratic nominee, whether he be for judicial or administrative office, without exception, and will work for harmony and peace. They will have my cooperation, and I shall expect their cooperation in return.

I am very sorry that the State Democratic Executive Committee did not consider me a good Democrat, but if I am permitted I will show it – that I am just as loyal a Democrat as ever lived. In fact, I have always insisted that this was a family row. I have frowned upon, and would not tolerate, a negro vote coming in to settle a Democratic fuss.

You have honored me by your vote, and whether you be Catholic or Protestant, gambler or saint, rich or poor, you will receive fair and considerate treatment at my hand.

I have no enemies to punish, and the people will find that my policy will be a broad, liberal and just one. It would be ridiculous for anyone to believe that I would even attempt to force religious views upon the body politic. I would rather have the people of the state to know at the beginning that my policy will be broad, philanthropic and for the best interest of all concerned, and that no sumptuary or blue laws of New England will ever find a place in my administration.

People of Florida, now that the Governorship has been decided by you, it is best that we forget all differences and let the cordial spirit of cooperation permeate our great State.

I shall meet all in the spirit of fairness and as I shall meet you on that basis I shall expect to have the same treatment.

Sidney J. Catts.

Having offered a handkerchief to those whom noses he had just bloodied, Catts believed that all the bitterness of the campaign would fade. He naïvely thought the Democratic establishment would line up behind him and forgive him due to his pledge to be a "good Democrat." He was mistaken.

20. Taking Office

ONE of the things that drew voters to Catts was that he knew how to put on a show. His inauguration on January 2, 1917 gave him the opportunity to impress and beguile the Crackers once more before he settled into the Governor's Mansion and became Florida's conscientious Chief Executive.

One thing that hampered Catts was his chronic lack of funds. He and his close family could not even afford proper attire for the event. A friend and supporter, Joe Earman, publisher of *The Palm Beach Post*, came to the rescue. Earman provided the Catts family funds to purchase clothes for the inauguration. In addition, Earman wrote the Governor-elect a $48 check for a new suit.

The new Governor desired to prove that he was progressive. One thing he did to prove he was forward looking was by replacing the traditional horse-drawn buggies with two hundred automobiles for the inaugural parade. Catts rode in the lead car, a Model T that sported a sign reading "THIS IS THE CAR THAT GOT ME HERE."

In addition, Catts made sure that a film crew recorded the inauguration. It marked the first inauguration in Florida thus recorded. While the above items were largely symbolic, they made a great impact upon those whom Catts identified as his natural constituents.

As Catts stood before the large, noisy crowd of 5,000 attending his inaugural, he must have felt that he had finally made it.

Catts also continued to enthrall his supporters with his words during his inaugural address. He told his Crackers, "Your triumph is no less in this good hour in beautiful Florida, for you have withstood the onslaughts of the county and state political rings, the corporations, the railroads, the fierce opposition of the press and organization of the Negro voters of this state against you and the power of the Roman Catholic hierarchy against you. Yet over all of these the common people of Florida, the everyday cracker people have triumphed."

In addition, Catts remained true to his fundamentalist values. While the state threw a lavish inaugural ball for him, Catts refused to attend because he was morally opposed to dancing.

By most accounts, Catts was off to a great start. He believed that could not help but to succeed. Governor Catts was mistaken.

The first sign of trouble came at the Catts inauguration. The Justices of the Florida State Supreme Court, Democrats all, refused to take their designated places in the inaugural parade until W. W. Flournoy the attorney for Catts pleaded with them to do so.

One thing about Catts was that he was in many ways one of the "Crackers" he claimed to represent. When he moved into the Governor's

Mansion, he brought with him a milk cow, several pigs, and a large number of chickens.

Catts was still a Democrat in his own mind, but the Florida Democratic establishment disowned him and determined to hobble him and his agenda. The establishment's opposition was not merely political. Catts presented an agenda that was distastefully progressive to many of Florida's legislators.

Some of the specific measures Catts supported included:

(1) Enactment of statewide Prohibition

(2) Enactment of the Federal Aid Road Act

(3) Imposition of an Inheritance Tax

(4), Creation of a State Tax Commission

(5) Improved Vocational Education

(6) Simplification of election laws,

(7) Taxation of church property, except for the church and pastor's home

(8) Opening closed institutions

(9) Same school license for public, private, and denominational schoolteachers

(10) The drainage of Everglades

(11) Increased pensions for old soldiers

(12) The creation of a Seminole Reservation

(13) The enactment of a Flag Law for the State

(14) Enactment of a benefit tax on right to hold large bodies of land

(15) Creation of a bank guarantee fund

(16) Enactment of laws favoring labor unions

(17) Building better shipping facilities for the producer

(18) Taxing corporations based on their gross receipts, not their profits

(19) Laws lowering legal rate of interest

(20) Catts called for full suffrage and equal rights for women and he was one of the first American governors to appoint a woman to his staff.

Despite severe opposition from the Florida legislature, Catts, as we will see, got a considerable of his agenda enacted into law.

21. The Bigot Governor

SIDNEY J. Catts was not the only Florida politician to campaign on a platform of intolerance, far from it. For instance, in 1916, Park Trammell defeated incumbent United States Senator Nathan P. Bryan in the contest for the Democratic nomination largely because Bryan had supported the appointment of a Roman Catholic postmaster in Jacksonville.

The difference with Catts is that he maintained, and continued to spout those positions throughout his tenure as Florida's 22nd Governor. However, it is clear that he intended some of his strongest rhetoric to be nothing more than red meat for his followers to devour. However, in some instances, it indicated a deep hatred for those he attacked.

Even though President Wilson had campaigned on the slogan, "He Kept us Out of War" as soon as the election was over, Wilson began to push for American entrance into the conflict and on April 6, 1917, the United States declared war on Germany and the other Central Powers.

While many felt appalled and dismayed by America sending troops across the "Great Pond" that was the Atlantic Ocean to fight in the European war "to end all wars," Catts saw it as a political opportunity.

Catts stirred up anti-German and anti-Roman Catholic sentiment throughout his campaign for Governor and the war afforded him the opportunity to continue, and even ratchet up his rhetoric while he was Governor. Ignoring the restraints most holding high office feel, Catts openly speculated about things about which he had no credible information.

Governor Catts publicly repeated the conspiracy theory he had first postulated while a candidate that the monks of St. Leo Abbey were in cahoots with the Germans. Many of the monks were German-Americans or German immigrants and Catts claimed that they were making plans to arm Florida's African American population and then to direct the African Americans in a rebellion in support of Kaiser Wilhelm II.

After the successful revolution, the Kaiser would put Pope Benedict XV in charge of Florida, and the Pope would move the Holy See to a small town north of Tampa called San Antonio, Florida and shut down all of the Protestant churches in the Sunshine State.

Anti-German reaction in Florida was already strong due to the war fever fanned by Wilson in Washington and Catts only enflamed the situation further. Fearful of physical attacks, many German immigrants decided to move out of Florida and settle elsewhere in the United States. This was just fine by Catts. He saw "Germans" leaving as a positive for the Sunshine State.

Catts did not see all his anti-Catholic allegations go unchallenged, however. Right Reverend Charles Mohr, the Abbot of St. Leo, published several refutations to the conspiracy theories bandied about by Catts. Additionally, a good number of Protestants went out of their way to appear in public with local Catholics in Pasco County and elsewhere. Faced with opposition, Catts didn't back down from his previous remarks, but he did tone down his statements.

Yet, despite all his anti-Catholic statements, Catts did not really hate Catholics – at least, he didn't show hatred for individual Catholics. He hired a Roman Catholic as his secretary. Additionally, Catts did not object when his son, Rozier, married a Roman Catholic.

However, when it came to African Americans, Catts was not just a demagogue preaching racism for political effect, he was a dedicated hater. In fact, he had no problem stating his believe that African Americans were an "inferior race" in public.

When the NAACP criticized the lynching of two African American men, Catts refused to condemn the hangings. On the contrary, he penned a scathing response denouncing the NAACP specifically and African Americans generally. Catts wrote, "Your Race is always harping on the disgrace it brings to the state by a concourse of white people taking revenge for the dishonoring of a white woman, when if you would . . . [teach] your people not to kill our white officers and disgrace our white women, you would keep down a thousand times greater disgrace."

Another time, the American Civil Liberties Union (ACLU) asked Governor Catts to investigate the hanging of four blacks in North Florida and Catts penned a hateful response.

Catts wrote, "When Negro men get drunk and kill white men in the U.S., or especially in the South, or lynch or ravish or rape white women they will certainly be hung or shot and if the fools would learn to stop doing these things our people will stop taking revenge on them."

Yet, even when dealing with African Americans Catts was inconsistent. During his term he blasted African Americans for being a criminal race, yet, he appointed an African American to the position as a parole officer in Duval County.

Catts went out of his way to insult other ethnic groups as well. During a dispute, he stated that he would suspend a Duval County (Jacksonville) Sheriff "as quick as I would a guinea nigger." The term Catts used was a common slur employed towards Italian Americans used in those days, but virtually no Governor would use it or the "N" word in public for that matter.

22. The Spoils System

𝒫ATRONAGE (the Spoils System) had been around nationally since Thomas Jefferson replaced all the Federalists he could when he became President. Of course, every state also practiced patronage. However, state Governors usually followed a few rules in applying the Spoils System. First, they tried to ensure that those they appointed for political reasons were reasonably competent. Additionally, they retained brilliant bureaucrats without regard to politics. Catts did not follow those rules, nor did he display any tolerance toward those he feared might be disloyal to him. On several occasions, he dismissed officeholders for the most trivial reasons.

Catts went into office knowing that the Florida Constitution barred him from seeking reelection. However, he did not plan to serve out his term and then disappear into the long shadows of history. He intended to dominate Florida politics for years to come. He reasoned that the only way to accomplish this was to make use of the Democratic Party's political machine, or failing that, to build one of his own. From the beginning, the Florida Democratic leadership disowned Catts and he felt he had no choice except to manufacture a political machine from scratch.

Florida law helped Catts in building his political web. It gave him the authority to fill some 1,800 state jobs and he made the most of the opportunity afforded him. Catts fired literally hundreds of officeholders and replaced them with his cronies.

The truth is that a large percentage of those Catts fired were corrupt, some of them openly so. Catts removed Sheriffs in Monroe, Citrus, Clay, and Duval counties for offenses including tolerating prostitution, drunkenness on duty, and for "absence from the state." He discharged scores of local judges, county commissioners, tax collectors, and others. Catts justified the dismissals because the state auditor found widespread financial shortages among many county tax collectors.

The justifications Catts gave usually held up for the dismissals usually held up under scrutiny.

The truth was that "there were grounds for complaint in nearly every case." That was not the problem. One problem was that Catts replaced the ousted officials with his flunkies and many of them were just as corrupt as those they replaced. Another problem was that James B. Hodges used his newspaper in Lake City to "expose" officeholders less than completely loyal to Catts and ignoring the deeds of those in the Governor's pocket.

Catts didn't make some of the changes immediately. He first requested his opponents to resign, and if they didn't he would give them the boot. One notable person dismissed was Shellfish Commissioner, T. R. Hodges. Catts had promised that if elected, he would fire Hodges, and despite the Commissioner's promise that he follow the Governor's orders, Catts fired him anyway.

Some of those Catts cashiered held sway with the Florida legislature and lawmakers in Tallahassee passed "relief bills" to continue paying the ousted officials despite the fact that they were no longer working for the state. Catts tried to stop the relief bills, but many of them passed nonetheless.

During the 1919 legislative alone, lawmakers passed acts to reimburse a dozen fired officials more than $18,000 in lost salaries. One state representative even went so far as to propose a constitutional amendment designed to strip the Governor of the power to remove officeholders. The proposal reminded many to the infamous Tenure of Office Act passed by Congress during Reconstruction, and it failed.

For his part, Catts condemned those opposing his removing officeholders. He blamed the same combinations that he blamed for most other things: Catholics, newspapers, the courthouse ring, and the big corporations that he said had been dominating Florida for the past three decades.

Catts paid little attention to the quality of the applicants for the positions he was filling. Catts put James B. Hodges in charge of patronage and Hodges evaluated applicants on little more than their professed loyalty to Catts.

Hodges became the Governor's most trusted and most powerful advisor. Catts gave Hodges a free hand and in state hiring and no one who wanted a government job dared cross the Governor's aide.

Of course, Hodges wanted something for his help. Catts made sure that a fortune's worth of the state's legal business went to Hodges. This included pardon and parole cases. Beyond that, Catts appointed Hodges to the Board of Control and the State Plant Board. These boards involved higher education and plant diseases and Hodges benefitted from dishing out state contracts in connection with both of them.

Catts named J. V. Burke to be his Secretary at the hefty annual salary of $3,000. However, Burke had an eye aliment that forced him to resign from the position.

J. S. Blitch was a chief architect of the Catts victory at the polls and the Governor rewarded him by naming him State Tax Commissioner. When Burke resigned, Catts made Blitch his Secretary. In 1918, Catts appointed Blitch Superintendent of the State Prison Farm at Raiford.

Catts selected Jerry W. Carter to be the State Hotel Commissioner, but the opponents blocked him from assuming the office until 1919.

Catts gave Bryan Mack the well paying position as Secretary of the Board of Control, made Palm Beach newspaper publisher, Joe Earman, chairman, and the Governor's legal advisor, W. W. Flournoy, a Board member.

In the 1916 Democratic primary, J. Clifford R. Foster won the Democratic nomination for reappointment as Florida Adjutant General.

However, the primary was not binding and Catts turned Foster out. The Governor said that Foster's twelve years in office was long enough for any man to serve in any position and he said it was time for a change. Catts then appointed his political crony and old friend from his days in Alabama, J. B. Christian to the post. The new Adjutant General had made his living previously repairing watches.

Catts did gain some praise for appointing the highly qualified Attorney General, Thomas F. West to the Florida State Supreme Court. Catts then offered the job of Attorney General to his top flunky, Hodges. Hodges turned down the offer because he would have to stand for reelection in 1918 and he doubted that he could win it. Hodges reasoned that he was certain of a lucrative political job until 1921 by staying where he was and he saw no reason to jeopardize his position.

Catts then turned to the former Mayor of Jacksonville, Van Cicero Swearingen and named him State Attorney General. Swearingen won a full term in 1918. Swearingen, a rabid racist refused to prosecute any of those involved in the more than 50 murders by lynching that happened during his tenure. Swearingen did not seek reelection as Attorney General in 1920. Instead, Swearingen, running as a "Cattsist," unsuccessfully sought to win the Democratic nomination for Governor.

Governor Catts rewarded the manager of his Tampa Headquarters when he named W. H. Cox State Health Officer.

Catts turned to his South Florida campaign secretary, C. T. Frecker and made him Chairman of the State Board of Health.

Catts was not above nepotism either. He named his son-in-law, K. R. Paderick, Duval County tax collector.

When the Adjutant General's office came open again, the Governor named his son Sidney Catts, Jr. to the post.

Catts also had a job for his daughter, Ruth. He named her as his personal secretary to replace Blitch.

At one point, Catts family occupied no less than seven state positions. The payroll sheet read as follows:

Daughter, Governor's Private Secretary: Salary, $2,000
Daughter, Secretary to the State Board of Institutions: Salary, $ 1,000
Son, Naval Stores Inspector: Salary, $ 4,000
Son, Adjutant General: Salary, $ 3,000
Son, Harbor Master: Fees, $ 1,000
Son-in-law, Tax Collector of Duval County: Fees, $14,000
Governor: Salary, $ 6,000
Governor's contingent fund: $ 1,200
TOTAL: $32,200

Perhaps the most controversial of the Governor's appointments was that of his son, Sidney Johnston Catts, Jr. (1894-1969) to the position of Adjutant General.

The younger Catts was a student at the University of Florida when his father became Governor in 1917, but like many American youth, he developed War fever when the United States entered World War I. In April 1917, he abandoned his studies temporarily and joined the American Army. He received appointment to the first Officers Training Camp at Fort McPherson, Georgia and graduated with the rank of Second Lieutenant.

The younger Catts served in Europe from September 1918 and received his honorable discharge from the service on July 9, 1919. Although he was only twenty-five and he had limited military experience, Governor Catts appointed him Adjutant General on September 1, 1919.

Opponents of the Governor branded the appointment as nepotism pure and simple. It was a charge impossible to refute. There were numerous better-qualified persons in Florida and even the younger Catts was aware of it.

Despite his inexperience and the cloud he was under, Catts worked hard at being a competent Adjutant General. In the year he spent serving in the job, Catts organized thirteen companies of the Florida National Guard in thirteen different cities.

After leaving his job as Adjutant General, Catts, Jr. resumed his studies at the University of Florida and he gained his law degree in May 1922. However, the abuse he endured as Adjutant General soured him to government service. He never reentered the political arena.

By the time he left office, more than 100 members of the twenty-nine most important state boards owed their jobs to Catts. Additionally, during the final year of most administrations, there is a general stability in state jobs. This was not the case with Catts. During his final year, he continued to sweep out those of which he lacked faith. In 1919 and 1920, he forced fourteen resignations and suspended four other officeholders.

In fairness to Catts, some of his appointments performed their jobs well. However, this was more by accident than by design. Catts had no real executive experience and he instituted no system designed to find the most qualified candidates for state jobs. If he happened to appoint a qualified person, it was likely just a matter of dumb luck.

It is also true that Catts replaced some of those he appointed when proven hopelessly incompetent or egregiously corrupt. However, his motivations for firing them were hardly a result of his desire for good, honest, and effective government. Most of the removals came because of the public outcry when Florida's citizens learned of specific examples of incompetence or corruption.

Catts had talked a lot during his campaign for Governor about making Florida's public schools bastions of Protestantism. To this end the new Governor was especially interested in dominating the Florida Board of Control. The Board of Control operated the University of Florida, Florida State College for Women, the Florida School for the Deaf & Blind, and

Florida A & M College. Thus, the Board of Control had important influence over higher education in Florida.

The new Governor reasoned that if he dominated the Board of Control, he would dominate education in Florida as well. To accomplish his goal, Catts declined to reappoint the very popular P. K. Yonge of Pensacola to the Board. Yonge had chaired the Board of Control for many years and the only reason for removing him was political. With Yonge as chair, Catts would only have two of the five votes on the Board and could not influence it in the way he envisioned.

Yonge was not above playing politics himself. He sought to secure his position by moving that the Board elect him to another term as chair before Catts could act. However, retiring member Frank E. Jennings blocked the effort. He admonished Yonge for attempting to engage in the very shenanigans those opposing Catts said the new Governor intended to employ.

Several Presidents of the schools governed by the Board of Control feared that Catts would establish an educational dictatorship in Florida. University of Florida President A. A. Murphree wrote a colleague, "Ye Gods! Save the State from this horrible political autocracy."

Catts got his way and established the Board of Control he wanted. Earman served as Chair, Bryan Mack was Secretary, and James B. Hodges, H. J. Brett of DeFuniak Springs, and John B. Sutton of Tampa, served as members of the board. However, Catts did not establish anything approaching a dictatorship over the state's educational system. He grew disinterested in the Board of Control quickly and seldom interfered with it. The Board reflected the Catts philosophy that "classical education" had dubious value and that the state should stress vocational education. Other than that, the board acted independently of the Governor generally.

While those opposing Catts screamed about the Governor appointing his unqualified friends to high positions, they conceded that his doing so was perfectly legal, if not perfectly ethical.

For his part, Catts admitted freely that he practiced nepotism and handed out jobs as rewards for political favors. He continued that there was nothing wrong with the Spoils system and that it was a time-honored practice. Catts chastised the hypocrisy of his political adversaries for condemning him for doing what they had always done.

As described earlier, the party bosses among the Democrats refused to accept Catts and his patronage operation was one of political necessity as much as political expediency. Catts viewed patronage as a matter of political survival. The Governor realized he would have no political life beyond his one term as Governor if he did not build an organization strong enough to take on and overcome Florida's courthouse ring.

23. Catts and the Legislature

*T*HE truth is that the Florida economy was booming during the Catts era and the good times would last until the stock market crash of 1929. Yet, it is impossible to say that Catts did much to add to the prosperity the state enjoyed.

Despite the fact that Democratic Party controlled the Florida legislature when it convened in Tallahassee in April 1917, and that that Democratic leadership had declared war of the new Governor before he took office, there were many in the Sunshine State that desired to give the Catts a fair chance to succeed.

Oddly, some Florida newspapers were conciliatory, even accommodating towards the new administration. Willis M. Ball, publisher of Jacksonville's conservative *Florida Times-Union* offered to make his newspaper the "official organ" of the Catts administration. While the Governor and Ball never made any formal agreement, the paper remained sympathetic towards Catts and his legislative agenda.

Catts enlisted James B. Hodges to act as his liaison between the executive and the legislative branches and Hodges soon enlisted Senator M. L. Plympton and Representative W. J. Roebuck of Columbia County to align with Catts. Representative Arthur Gomez of Key West consented to sponsor the Governor's programs in the Florida House. A former classmate of Catts at Cumberland University Law School, State Senator James E. Alexander of DeLand agreed act as the Governor's whip in the Senate.

In his first message to the state legislature, Catts laid out his agenda. Lawmakers and ordinary citizens alike already knew the agenda, because it was virtually identical to the platform he had campaigned on across the state in 1916. Catts called for action on:

(1) Statewide Prohibition

(2) Abolition of the convict lease system by utilizing prisoners on state roads

(3) A graduated inheritance tax

(4) Enlarged power for the State Tax Commission to investigate large corporations, which were escaping taxation, properly

(5) Creation of industrial schools for the education of boys and girls

(6) Abolition of the Bryan Primary Law

(7) Adoption of initiative, referendum, and recall legislation

(8) Taxation of church property other than churches and parsonages

(9) Adoption laws to protect depositors from bank failures.

Catts also made an impassioned plea for prison reform. He proposed the creation of a state office dedicated to advocating for prison inmates. Catts said the "Friend of the Convict Office" would be a major step toward reducing crime in Florida. Catts also promised to pardon more inmates than had any of his predecessors had.

Catts kept his word and did pardon many convicted criminals. Some of the Governor's opponents suspected that he and his cronies had traded pardons for bribes, but no evidence of bribery related to pardons ever emerged.

Catts also supported the "One Man, One Vote" principle decades before the Supreme Court ruled on the subject. In 1917, he called for reapportionment to stop the inequality resulting from the overrepresentation of rural counties.

In the first few weeks of his term, Catts received high marks from much of Florida's newspapers. For instance, the *Gainesville Sun* reported, "The chief executive is better posted concerning conditions in Florida than many supposed him to be."

However, the opinion of newspaper editors meant little to the Democratic leaders. They fought to defeat virtually everything Catts proposed. The legislature refused to act on reapportionment, and education. Then it voted to abolish the State Tax Commission and defeated efforts at labor reform.

James B. Hodges was an effective lobbyist for the Governor, but only when he agreed with the legislation he was peddling. Hodges did quality in the effort to pass the Bank Guarantee Bill, but did almost nothing on the issue of tax reform.

Hodges was close to attorney J. E. Hall. Hall was the General Counsel for the powerful Georgia Southern and Florida Railroad. The relationship, whether friendly or professional, was the driving force in Hodges advising Governor Catts that the railroads were already paying their fair share and that increasing their tax burden would damage the state.

In April of 1917, after talks with Catts, Hodges happily informed Hall that the new Governor had no "disposition to urge any legislation that would be adverse to us, except the enlargement of the powers of the Tax Commission . . . ." Hodges continued that he was certain that Catts was sympathetic to the railroads on "organized labor bills."

As stated above, not only would the legislature not enact the Governor's plan to enlarge the scope and powers of the Tax Commission, it voted to kill it. Catts refused to allow the Tax Commission to go away without a fight. He vetoed the bill abolishing the Commission and the State House upheld the veto 37 to 31.

Catts also vetoed a bill abolishing the State Railroad Commission.

In his first year in office, Catts failed to get much through the legislature, but he did have some important successes. He secured the sale of the *Roamer* as he promised he would. He also secured a provision for a statewide referendum on liquor sales and the creation of state industrial schools.

However, Catts spent most of his first year in office on the defensive. Among the acts he vetoed was the "two-primary law." Catts felt the two-primary law was even more complicated and even less workable than the election law that had caused him to have the Democratic primary stolen from him in 1916.

The legislature and Catts also butted heads on state appointments. As stated earlier, the legislature, much to the dismay of the Governor, passed several acts to pay the salaries of state officials dismissed by Catts.

Catts called for reconciliation with the Democratic establishment, but he wasn't about to knuckle under to the party bosses. At the end of the 1917 legislative session, he rewarded his most faithful lieutenants. Catts made State Representative W. J. Roebuck State Convict Inspector. Then the Governor named State Senator James Alexander Judge of the Seventh Judicial District. Additionally, Catts appointed State Representative Arthur Gomez County Solicitor for Monroe County.

Finding much of his program stalled, Catts decided to break the logjam in the legislature. On November 15, 1918, he called the legislature in special session. The stated purpose of the special session was to implement the newly adopted Prohibition amendment to Florida's Constitution. The Prohibition Party's support of Catts paid off in a big way. In 1917, the first year of the Catts regime and three years before Prohibition swept across the nation, Florida enacted law prohibiting the manufacture, sale or use of alcoholic beverages. (Most Floridians obeyed the law.)

Yet, the Prohibitionists felt betrayed by Catts on another front. The Prohibition Party had always opposed state-sponsored gaming in any form, and many Prohibitionists felt shocked when they learned that Catts supported giving Florida communities the option of allowing gambling.

Catts had more in mind when he called the special session than just getting an enabling act through the legislature on Prohibition. He intended to win over the Democratic majority, finally.

During the special session, Catts changed course and embraced the idea abolishing the State Tax Commission. His stated the reason for his reversal was that in some counties, the Commission allowed very low tax assessments while allowing much higher tax assessments in other counties.

The Governor also reversed himself on the State Railroad Commission and called for its abolition. Catts contended that abolishing the Railroad Commission would save the state $70,000 annually. Catts did not point out that Florida's big railroads wanted the Commission abolished desperately.

Although Catts won approval for his desired Prohibition enforcement laws and the abolishment of the Tax Commission, the legislature refused to destroy the Railroad Commission.

During the regular session of the Florida legislature in 1919, Catts returned to some of his earlier proposals and added a few new ones – with mixed results. The Governor's agenda was comprehensive, and although many of those things he wanted had no chance of passage, he did win some battles in the legislature. Some of the items Catts pushed for in 1919 included:

(1) The federal repeal of the espionage acts which inhibited free speech

(2) University extension education to reduce adult illiteracy

(3) The equalization of property taxation

(4) A franchise tax on corporations (This item caused the big railroads and other large companies to condemn Catts and to work for his political opponents.)

(5) A state inheritance tax

(6) Stronger legislation protecting child laborers

(7) A workman's compensation law

(8) The creation of a State Bureau of Labor Statistics

(9) Compulsory universal education through the eighth grade

(10) Placement of a ceiling on interest rates charged by loan companies

Again, James B. Hodges took on the difficult role as the chief lobbyist for the Administration. Additionally, the Governor's pet newspaper, the *Florida Times-Union*, ran editorials enthusiastically endorsing most of the agenda Catts proposed.

Catts lost most of his battles with the legislature, but he did win some impressive victories in 1919.

Wins Catts achieved in 1919 included:

(1) Abolishing the convict lease system

(2) Reform of the state prison system

(3) Legislation aimed at improving highways

(4) Educational reform

Catts had an especial passion for improving prison conditions in Florida. He visited several prisons and reform schools, including the State Prison Farm in Raiford. Catts appointed J. S. Blitch to run Raiford who made it a roaring success.

Determined to transform Raiford into a national model for prison reform, in a mere nine months, Blitch doubled prison revenue, and halved prison expenditures. He cashiered forty paid guards and replaced them with fourteen prisoners that he gave the title of "foremen." With prisoners in charge, there were no escapes. Blitch also made prisoners crew leaders, office personnel, and security officers. Overall, these "trustees" performed their duties exceptionally.

Beyond that, Blitch provided prisoners with recreational activities, ball fields, and an auditorium. Not only were Blitch's reformed unheard of in Florida before, few prisons anywhere in America could boast of anything approaching the quality and humanity of the Raiford Prison Farm. Blitch earned the reputation as "one of the outstanding prison superintendents in the United States."

With his successes at Raiford, Catts saw an opportunity to realize two other of his pet projects: (1) end the convict lease system and (2) improve Florida roadways. Catts got behind a bill to use Raiford prisoners to build and maintain state roads. The bill called for Florida to accept $3 million in federal funds while spending another $3 million in state money. In order to raise the state's share, Florida would use convicts for the work and would add two tenths of one cent (2 mills) to the state sales tax. After a long debate, the legislature passed the proposal into law.

Catts also took pleasure in ramming education bills through the legislature. Joe Earman proposed that Florida initiate a university extension program designed to educate citizens of the state who could not attend regular college classes. Catts worked diligently to promote the idea and in 1919, the legislature passed the Turnbull University Extension Act and allocated $50,000 to fund it.

Catts and Earman also successfully worked together to get the legislature to add $250,000 back to the Board of Control's budget that it had cut earlier. This increased the Board's budget back to the $800,000 it had requested.

Another important education measure Catts got through the legislature was a bill making school attendance for Florida child between six and sixteen mandatory. While some farming families did not want to take their sons out of the fields to learn to read and write, most Floridians observed the new law without serious complaint.

Due largely to the educational reforms Catts championed, by 1920, school attendance in Florida had increased by 52.1% from 1910. In raw numbers, the increase was from 148,089 students in 1910 to 225,160 in 1920. Without the insistence of Catts for reform, most of those 77,071 students reflected by the increase would not have attended school but would have lived their lives illiterate.

Catts was a big spender and big spenders always increase taxes, Other than the tax increases already mentioned, Catts succeeded in getting a constitutional amendment allowing the taxation of intangible property.

The Governor also felt gratified by obtaining the passage of a child welfare bill and the creation of the Florida Farm Colony for Epileptic and Feeble Minded.

Yet, Catts suffered several setbacks too. The legislature rejected the Governor's plan for (1) the ratification of a constitutional amendment mandating woman suffrage in Florida, (2) for reapportionment of State House and Senate districts, (3) for fair labor legislation, and for bank guarantees on deposits. Yet, considering everything, Catts enjoyed a very successful year in 1919.

The truth is that although Catts saw much of his program passed, the victories were in because of him as much as they were in spite of him. The majority of Florida's legislators felt repulsed by Catts. He was not the courtly or gentlemanly kind of Governor they desired. They never forgave him for embarrassing the Democratic Party establishment in November 1916. Finally, he had usurped the political machine operated by the Democratic Party and had created his own patronage system.

Yet, Catts still deserves credit for championing many reforms. He may have been more popular had he been less adamant about supporting measures in opposition to views of most Floridians, but all reformers risk the ire of those resistant to change.

24. The End of Cattsism

*T*HE term, "Cattsism," applied (often in derision) to the principles and statements of Governor Catts. Catts was a polarizing figure. With him, there was no middle ground. His opinions seemed set in stone. He quickly developed a cult following and his admirers, especially in the Florida panhandle, were willing to go to almost any end to see his proposals made into law. There Cattsists would also brave almost any weather extreme to vote for Catts.

On the other hand, many Floridians detested Catts. These anti-Cattsists were just as fervent in their opposition to him as the Cattsists were in supporting him. The anti-Cattsists promised to spare no effort in defeating his followers in 1920 elections. They also intended to end the political career of Sidney J. Catts permanently.

Catts could not succeed himself as Governor in 1920, but he was not finished with politics. The only decision for him was on the office he wished to seek. He soon set his eyes upon the United States Senate. It was one of the worse political blunders of his life.

Catts could have avoided seeking any office in 1920, tried to behave like a good, partisan solder, get in the good graces of the Democratic Party, and after rehabilitating himself within the looked to run for some other office to seek down the road. However, he did not intend to do that. He could have sought a seat in Congress, but there was not a seat available to him. He could have made a run at a Florida legislative office, but that did not appeal to him either. Catts could have even sought the 1920 Presidential nomination on either the Democratic Party Ticket or that of a Third Party. However, even Catts did not possess an ego big enough for him to delude himself into believing that he was presidential timber.

Catts felt his best option was to attempt to unseat popular United States Senator, Duncan Upshaw Fletcher in the 1920 Democratic Primary. While he undoubtedly knew the odds were long, Catts took comfort from the fact that he had accomplished the impossible before.

Catts may have made his choice to go after Fletcher because of his personal dislike for the Senator. Fletcher had made a strong effort to defeat Catts in 1916, and the Governor never forgave him for it. On the contrary, Catts desired to punish the Senator for opposing him so vociferously during the gubernatorial campaign. The idea of knocking Fletcher from his lofty perch was too tempting for Catts to resist.

As early 1917, Catts allowed rumors to spread that he was considering a run for the Senate and then in 1919, fresh off his limited legislative successes, Catts began stirring towards a Senate run. On June 16, 1919, Catts made it official as he announced his intention to seek the Senate seat. However, he soon learned what a difficult a task he faced. As stated earlier, Fletcher was popular and the Democratic establishment was behind him. Beyond that, many leaders in the Democratic Party held a searing hatred towards Catts. They would have supported anyone over the Governor in the primary. Some would have even endorsed a Republican to keep Catts out of Washington.

Yet, Catts felt he could defeat the elitist Democrats again by appearing to the "common man" and the Florida Cracker. For instance, Catts had a good record with organized labor. In 1919, 3,500 phosphate workers in Polk County went on strike and Catts defended them against the "big business" interests opposing their union.

Additionally, Catts tried to build a political machine for his whole term. He truly believed he could fashion a statewide organization in Florida strong enough to defeat the apparatus maintained by the courthouse ring. However, Governor Catts had decimated his organization as quickly as he built it. Catt had a volatile nature and his quick temper and childish pettiness had driven many of his own allies away from him before 1920. Catts was easily outraged and he was subject to firing officials, even politically powerful allies at the slightest provocation. Of course, those he cashiered were not eager to help him ever again. In fact, a good number of his former cronies actively worked his opponent in 1920.

Of his 1916 allies, the governor had dismissed State Health Officer W. H. Cox for malfeasance of office. While the firing may have been justified, the loss of Cox's support damaged Catts in West and South Florida.

Catts fired the Chairman of the State Board of Health C. T. Frecker for being a disruptive influence. Frecker's loss was a blow to Catts in South Florida.

Catts fired his old friend, Adjutant General J. B. Christian for refusing to carry out the Governor's orders. The firing made others in the Governor's inner circle nervous. If Catts would fire a childhood chum, they reasoned, no one was safe from the wrath of Catts.

Catts replaced Adjutant General Christian with James McCants. McCants had been an early supporter of Catts, but he became disenchanted and he resigned from office when Catts refused to stop interfering with his decisions.

The legal brains behind the Catts campaign for Governor, W. W. Flournoy became more than a disillusioned advisor; he became an outright enemy of the Governor's. Flournoy openly worked to help prevent Catts from gaining the Senate nomination in 1920.

W. W. Phillips became enraged with Catts over the Governor's handling of the State Board of Health and he too became an enemy of the Red-haired demagogue. Phillips had influence in Columbia County and breaking with Phillips cost Catts votes there.

Catts exploded with anger when he learned of rumors that W. J. Roebuck drank whiskey on a regular basis. The rumor was untrue, but the Governor made a scene and came within an eyelash of removing Roebuck from his position as State Convict Inspector. After Catts learned the truth, he allowed Roebuck to remain on the job, but the two men were never close again.

Despite the fact that he was facing an entrenched incumbent, that the Democratic kingmakers were aligned against him, and that his own organization in disarray, Catts entered the contest with the blind confidence of prophet and the blind courage of a martyr. If he doubted that he would win, he never let on.

Senator Fletcher was a large, debonair man, and by 1920, he was bald. Like Catts, Fletcher took his law degree from a Tennessee law school. Fletcher's L. L. B. came from Vanderbilt University in 1881.

Like Catts, Fletcher was inconsistent when it came to the Race issue. Fletcher, at times behaved as racist as did Catts. The Senator expressed his view when he spoke about the Civil War. He told audiences, "The South fought to preserve race integrity . . . We fought to maintain free white domination." Fletcher left no doubt that he agreed with those goals.

On the other hand, Fletcher sometimes expressed a pro-equality attitude. For instance, in 1896, he successfully pushed to have the Florida bar admit James Weldon Johnson. Thus, Johnson became the first African American to gain a law license by examination in Florida.

Fletcher was a better attorney than was Catts and he was very successful at arguing court cases. He was successful in politics as well. When Fletcher first entered politics, he aligned himself with the reform faction of the Democratic Party that called itself the "Straight-out Democrats." However, over time, Fletcher affiliated with the conservative faction of the party by the late 1890s and he was under the thumb of the big business, especially the railroad companies.

Fletcher worked his way up the political ladder. He served on the Jacksonville City Council, in the Florida State House, and two separate terms as Mayor of Jacksonville. Fletcher also chaired the Board of Public Instruction of Duval County and was President of the Gulf Inland Waterways Association. In 1905, he became the Counsel for the Florida East Coast Railroad.

Fletcher's next step up the political ladder was in 1905 when he became the chair of the Florida State Democratic Executive Committee. He held the post until 1908.

Appointed to the United States Senate in 1909, he won reelection in 1914, 1920, 1926, and 1932. Fletcher died in office in 1936.

Senator Fletcher made many of promises to the people of Florida before he went to the nation's capital. He called for a federal income tax, tough regulation of trusts and monopolies, tariff reductions, and federal revitalization of waterways and harbors. However, Fletcher was not crusader or a troublemaker. He went to Washington determined to be a good soldier for the Democratic Party. When Woodrow Wilson took office in 1913, Fletcher became one of the President's strongest supporters.

Catts understood that an early start was imperative for an underdog and he hit the campaign trail as quickly as was feasible for him. The Governor hopped in his Ford automobile and headed out across the state. Catts was certain that he could win on the same issues that put him in the Governor's Mansion in 1916. Catts did not attempt to adjust his tactics. He didn't use advance men or develop a preplanned itinerary. He would just drive to a small town, jump out of the car, and start giving a stem-winding speech of the kind that had made him famous.

Catts had virtually no support among newspapers and he knew he could not count on the press to give him any help at all. Instead, he had his agents print up colorful circulars like those that stores, shops, and travelling circuses distributed. The circulars proved to be much more effective than his opponents thought they would be.

By the time the calendar flipped over to January 1920, the Catts Senate campaign was in high gear and it appeared that the Governor would give the Senator a run for his money. Some even speculated openly that Catts might pull off another miracle. The strong early campaign mounted by Catts worried Fletcher and his aides. Despite this, the Senator's reelection campaign got off to a much slower start than he had planned.

Everyone knew that Fletcher was seeking reelection but the didn't issue a formal announcement until March 5, 1920. During his statement, Fletcher bragged happily about his experience and seniority. The Senator pointed out that he was the eighth ranking Democrat in the US Senate and that if the Democrats won control of the upper House in 1920, he stood to become the chair of the powerful Senate Commerce Committee. Additionally, he would have broad influence as a member of the Democratic Steering Committee. According to Fletcher, the possibility of both those happy occurrences boded well for Florida.

Fletcher had hoped to be back in Florida in early March to begin campaigning, but the bitter battle over American entrance into the League of Nations twice caused him to delay his return to Florida. Fletcher supported President Wilson's push to have America enter the League, but there wasn't any real chance of winning on the issue and Fletcher left Washington to begin personal campaigning for reelection just as soon as the Senate rejected America's entrance into the League.

Fletcher left Washington on March 20 with the promise that he would campaign every day until the June 8 Democratic Primary. Fletcher left no doubt that he intended to defeat Catts and render Cattsism a bad memory – a figment of Florida's past.

Fletcher kicked off his campaign on March 26, 1920 at a Farmers' Union meeting, inside a little country school near Ocala. The Senator wanted to appear to be calm and dignified throughout his campaign. He felt this poster would make for a favorable contrast between him and Catts. Fletcher didn't say much about politics during his kickoff speech. The Senator spoke of how important farmers were to Florida and the nation. He pointed out that farmers had benefited from the farm loan bank that he initiated. However, Fletcher told the audience that the Florida farmer "was not reaping the full reward of his toil" and he implied that Catts was to blame for it.

On March 27, Fletcher spoke in the courtroom at Live Oak, Florida. The Senator's handlers sought to create a spectacle of the type Catts was famous. Two airplanes engaged by the Live Oak Chamber of Commerce accompanied the train that carried Fletcher to Live Oak from Jacksonville.

Evidently not satisfied with his speech to the farmers, Fletcher decided to sling a little mud. He attacked Catts on his record (Fletcher distorted that record a bit) and criticized the Governor for canvassing across the state instead of seeing to his gubernatorial duties in Tallahassee.

The Senator again praised his farm measure. He added praise of the Merchant Marine Act when he had a part in passing. He said that the Merchant Marine Act offered substantial benefits to Florida.

Fletcher was, at best, a fair speaker. He had none of the fire of Catts and made no real effort to out preach Catts. Fletcher often reminded voters that he was a Washington insider and that if they would send him back to the Senate, he would work for federal benefits of all sorts for Florida. However, Fletcher spent more time attacking Catts than he did of praising himself.

Fletcher went out of his way to attack the patronage system Catts employed and the undeniable nepotism Catts practiced. Fletcher denounced turning qualified and honest persons out of office and replacing them with unqualified persons simply for political reasons or because they were members of the Catts family.

However, Fletcher's wide-ranging charges of "gross nepotism" contained several gross misrepresentations as well. According to Fletcher, the nepotism brought into the coffers of the first family of the state no less than $32,200 a year in salary and fees. However, $6,000 in state monies Fletcher counted included the Governor's annual salary. Another $1,200 was the Governor's contingent fund. Thus, at least one-quarter of the monies from the alleged "gross nepotism" had no connection to the appointment of the Governor's relatives.

The attack on Catts for campaigning for another office while still serving as Governor evidently scored some points with voters. Catts hater, Judge William B. Young wrote to the *Florida Times-Union* floating the idea of a amendment to the Florida Constitution that would prohibit any person from seeking another office while serving as Governor.

Cary A. Hardee, a candidate for Governor, and a Catts hater, promised that he would not seek any other office while serving as Governor. What Hardee did not say was that there was no United States Senate race scheduled in 1924, thus, Hardee could not have sought a Senate seat even if he had wished to make such a run.

Fletcher also attacked Catts for doubling the Florida tax rate. However, the attack against higher taxes was so cynical that it didn't score well with very many with knowledge of the situation. Yes, Catts was a big spender, but so was Fletcher. In fact, Fletcher, who was a strong supporter of the individual income tax, even conceded that Florida had needed tax increases between 1917 and 1920. When called out about his views on taxes after he attacked Catts, Fletcher answered timidly that he was careful with his own money.

Four years in office did nothing to diminish the ability of Catts to whip up a crowd, regardless of the weather. On February 5, Catts spoke in terrible weather outside the Madison, Florida courthouse to a surprisingly large number of citizens. Catts chose to open by pointing some of his successes. He spoke of the vast improvements in the conditions of the state prisons, hospitals, and industrial schools since he took office. At one point, Catts held up his hand and showed off a beautiful ring given to him at Christmastime 1919 by prisoners at the Raiford Prison Farm in gratitude for the implementation of the honor system in that institution.

Then, Catts went negative. The Governor denounced Woodrow Wilson for trying to force the United States into entangling alliances through the League of Nations. Catts continued that Washington was in a mess and he promised to clean it up just as he had cleaned up the state of Florida.

During this speech, Catts restrained himself from his usual bitter assault on the Church of Rome. However, Catts did take a few jabs at Catholics and he predicted that he would lose Escambia County because of the large Catholic population of Pensacola.

At other times, Catts painted Fletcher as a hopeless reactionary. The Governor pilloried his opponent for opposing stronger child labor laws. Catts mocked Fletcher for sponsoring the Guam Bill. Catts said the Guam Bill would have, if passed, transformed the tiny island land into a penal colony for "anarchists and reds."

As the campaign moved along, Catts increased his attacks against Catholics, but they never rose to the level to the 1916 campaign. He was especially moderate when he addressed crowds in Florida's largest of cities.

Amazingly, the same newspapers that attacked Catts for his anti-Catholic statements attacked him just as strongly because he appointed a Catholic to serve as Sheriff of Brevard County. One pundit wrote, "It is stated that Governor Catts has appointed a Catholic sheriff of Brevard county. Is this a change of front and does it mean that entirely different tactics will be employed in the approaching campaign?" Another wrote, "Perhaps the governor is hedging."

Catts wasn't concerned about any negative reaction that the appointment of a Catholic Sheriff might cause. His position was that the Roman Catholic Church, as an organization was the problem, not individual Catholics. In fact, he was so unconcerned about appointing the Sheriff that when Fletcher's allies attacked him on the issue, he ignored them.

However, another appointment the Governor made did concern him to the degree that he felt the need to give an explanation. Catts had made what he considered a major political blunder in appointing an African American as a Probation Officer in Duval County. The Governor apologized for his mistake, and reiterated that he was a confirmed racist. Then he retold the story of his killing an African American in Alabama and receiving an acquittal for it.

The Governor caused another controversy by his comments about what the press dubbed the "Camp Wheeler Affair." Catts stated several times during the campaign that on one occasion during wintertime, he visited Camp Wheeler, a National Guard training post near Macon, Georgia. Catts told horrified crowds that while he was at Camp Wheeler, he found several thousand Floridians suffering from pneumonia. Catts continued that the medical personnel were guilty of neglecting and improperly caring for the sick at the camp. In his booming voice, Catts bellowed that hundreds of the Florida boys he saw were either dead or dying. The claims made by Catts rang true because during World War I, a Spanish Flu pandemic struck the United States and thousands American soldiers died from the disease.

Catts then told his audiences that he had taken heroic measures to make sure the

Floridians received proper care. He claimed he had taken a train to Washington in the dead of winter in his efforts to save the boys. Catts related that he braved blizzard like conditions and stood knee-deep in snow while he sent telegrams to the proper authorities. Catts then beamed as he told his audiences that because of his pressure, the Floridians soon began to receive proper treatment and most of them survived.

After Catts related his Camp Wheeler story several times to several different crowds, Fletcher responded. The Senator said that Catts was not telling the truth about Camp Wheeler. The Senator stated categorically that Catts "was not in Washington at all that winter, and there never was a time when snow was knee deep on the streets, much less on the sidewalks, for one day in Washington, and there is surely no need to hunt snow banks in which to send telegrams."

Then, Fletcher provided an alternate version of what happened at Camp Wheeler. The Senator conceded that some died at the camp, but he said he had documented evidence that the total number of deaths at Camp Wheeler "only" amounted to 240 and of those "only" 48 were from Florida. Fletcher then said that he, not Catts, forced the Department of War to take action to act to rectify the situation at Camp Wheeler and to make sure that the Florida boys received quality care.

The two candidates also sparred over which deserved credit for preventing the Federal Government from establishing a leper colony on an island off Florida's coast. Each candidate continued to claim he prevented the leper colony all the way to the primary.

The fact that the Governor failed to build a strong machine did him more damage than his opponent did. Of course, Florida's Democrat regulars were all in for Fletcher. Neither could Catts build very much support from Florida newspapers. One reason, other than the fact that the owners of most papers were partisan Democrats, was that they felt that Fletcher was a friend of theirs. In a strong editorial, the *Macclenny Standard* explained why the newspapers supported Fletcher. The writer stated that the Senator was doing "more on behalf of the newspaper fraternity, by way of preventing the paper manufacturers from going still further with their profiteering antics, than any other individual in Washington . . ." The writer continued that the Senator's "efforts shall not be overlooked here in his home state."

Whether the editorial writer was sincere or not, the newspapers of Florida had opposed Catts from the time he announced for Governor in 1916. Other reasons why publishers opposed Catts were that (1) they were rich men and Catts was forever criticizing the rich, (2) they felt that Catts was not "respectable" or worse, that he was corrupt, and (3) that Catts put Florida in a bad light nationally and that kept new businesses from moving their operations to the Sunshine State.

The Senate contest between Catts and Fletcher drew national attention. The leftwing *Baltimore Sun* lined up in support of Fletcher.

In an unvarnished attack piece, the *Sun* related the opinion that if Catts won the primary "the current belief in the saving grace of democracy will receive an extremely severe shock. He is making . . . brutal and undisguised appeals to ignorance, prejudice and class feeling."

Yet, the editors did concede that Catts was speaking to a group of citizens that felt disaffected. While they contended that the Florida "Crackers" supporting Catts were ignorant and uneducated, they also contended that the Crackers were victims of abuse by the rich and by an uncaring state legislature. The newspapers claimed that a disreputable person like Catts could only gain power in Florida because respectable persons refused to treat the Crackers fairly.

Catts felt that the support of organized labor offered him a good opportunity to rekindle the fire of "working people" that warmed him to victory in 1916. Catts felt his campaign got a boost on February 8, 1920 when leaders of the American Federation of Labor in Washington announced that the organization intended to work in every political race in the United States to elect pro-labor candidates. A. F. L. head, Samuel Gompers promised that his group was and would remain non-partisan. He said his group was interested in electing "union men" regardless of party.

There was no doubt that Governor Catts had always been a friend of organized labor and that the A. F. L. felt that Fletcher was an enemy of their organization. The American Federation of Labor was especially angry with Fletcher because he voted to return the railroads to their private owners after World War I ended. Labor leaders had lobbied to nationalize the railroads permanently.

While organized labor did agree to support Catts eventually, that support was never more than lukewarm, and it came too late to do him much good. For his part, Catts made as strong a bid to gain the unequivocal support of organized labor in his bid to win the Democratic nomination. In one speech, the Governor said he had told his son, Sidney Catts, Jr., the Adjutant General, that if he ever ordered National Guardsmen to fire on a single striker, he would never put his foot under his father's table again.

However, Florida newspapers condemned Catts for his labor stances and some even accused Catts of stirring up labor unrest. On April 8, 1920, an unauthorized strike caused the spoliation of tons of fruits and vegetables. Sensing an opportunity, aids to Fletcher organized a rally in Jacksonville on May 25 condemning Catts as the sponsor of the unruly strikers.

During the rally, anti-Catts speakers condemned the involvement of organized labor in politics. Dr. Mark B. Herlong even went so far as to play the race card. He said that the American Federation of Labor was trying to achieve its ends, including securing the nomination for Catts, by qualifying African Americans to vote. It had to distress Catts that after all his years of unabashed racism, that his opponents would accuse him of using African Americans to gain a Senate seat.

Although Governor Catts desired the A. F. L. endorsement and he clearly deserved it, organized labor withheld its endorsement until the very last moment. Thus, Catts gained nothing from it. On the other hand, the Fletcher campaign used the Governor's currying for favor with big labor as "proof" that he was the "candidate of the Northern radicals, who brought about the railroad and dock strikes which resulted in stopping the shipment of fruits and vegetables, thereby causing the loss of hundreds of thousands of dollars."

We tend to think of trash talking among politicians as something new to politics. It is not. Fletcher drew loud and long laughter from a friendly audience at Avon Park when he cautioned them not to "swap a good horse in the middle of the stream for a jackass."

Catts drew similar laughter from a crowd in Winter Haven when he said he could prove he was more intelligent than his opponent was. Catts pointed out that he wore a larger hat than Fletcher did and that a larger hat meant a larger brain.

The Fletcher campaign also falsely accused Catts of saying that the Senator, who was a Unitarian, denied the divinity of Christ. A good many newspapers around Florida printed the lie as truth and it certainly cost Catts votes.

Catts told crowds that World War I veterans deserved rewards for their service. He suggested that it might be fitting to provide each veteran 40 acres of farmland and $100 cash for the harrowing service they provided in defense of their country.

Pro-Fletcher newspapers attacked Catts over the suggestion by comparing it to the attempts at equality employed by Republicans during the Reconstruction Period. On paper stated, "Catts reminds us of the carpetbaggers of the sixties who promised every darkey 40 acres of land and a mule. And we suppose he thinks our soldier boys are about on a par with the ignorant negroes of 50 years ago." Again, it was ironic that after his many racist speeches, his opponents would use racist slurs to attack him.

The candidates, both powerful men, had no problem using their positions to aid their campaigns. For instance, in Bronson on April 5, 1920, Fletcher interrupted a Grand Jury deliberation so he could deliver a speech in the crowded courtroom.

At Hastings, Catts interrupted a drilling National Guard unit and ordered it off the street so he could give a speech. Catts said of the Guardsmen, "They should know enough to show respect to the Governor."

The Catts campaign had started with nearly as much energy as his campaign for Governor had in 1916. However, by the time spring flowers began to bloom in 1920, it was clear that Catts was heading for an inglorious defeat.

Despite Fletcher's slow start and his uninspired speaking style, by April, he was drawing large, enthusiastic crowds and his confidence seemed to grow by the day. On the other hand, the Catts campaign was in disarray.

Agents of Senator Fletcher followed Catts around the state and heckled him during every speech he gave. It is interesting that a person of such powerful skill on the stump as Catts could not seem to handle the disruptions caused by the paid hecklers.

More importantly than the fleabites of the hecklers, Catts had to deal with sabotage within the ranks of his own campaign. One of his chief aides secretly conspired to prevent Catts from giving a speech at St. Petersburg by failing to secure the use of Williams Parks.

Catts also lost some of the groups that had supported him most strongly in 1916. Small fishing interests opposed the way the Catts Administration applied conservation laws.

As it began more and more apparent that Catts could not win the Democratic primary, his camp began to spread rumors that Catts might choose to run in November as a Prohibitionist, or as an independent. The establishment Democrats feared a repeat of 1916 and they sought a way to prevent Catts from continuing his campaign past the primary in June. In order to accomplish this, they set a trap for Catts.

During a debate at Wakulla Springs on May 1, Fletcher asked Catts directly if the Governor, who claimed that he had always been a Democrat, if he would abide by the primary result. Trapped, Catts knew that any hope he had of winning the primary would evaporate unless he pledged not to seek the Senate seat in November as an independent. Catts took a long drink of water, cleared his throat, and pledged to support the Democratic nominee for the Senate, no matter whom the nominee was.

As the days melted away and the primary drew closer, an overwhelming Fletcher victory grew more apparent. In fact, a Fletcher victory was so certain that, the violent newspaper assault on Catts diminished. Catts was no longer a threat and the pro-Fletcher forces felt it was to the Senator's advantage to try to unify the party and bring Crackers who adored Catts back into the mainstream of the Democratic Party. However, they did not attempt to welcome Catts back to them.

Knowing that the tide against him was fast becoming a tsunami, Catts sought desperately to turn the campaign around. He knew he needed a dramatic and dynamic issue to do it. His anti-Catholic pitch no longer helped him and his opponent was just as willing to play the race card as he was. With nothing else to stir the hearts of Florida voters, Catts tried to tie Fletcher to the trusts and monopolies that the Governor claimed were destroying working people. Catts offered that Fletcher had done nothing to curb the high cost of living or corporate profiteering because the Senator was a "corporation man." Despite the Governor's best efforts, the attacks had no effect.

As the results of the June 8 primary rolled in, the magnitude of the landslide suffered by

Catts and Cattsism soon became apparent. The result was:

Fletcher: 62,304 (71.4%)

Catts: 25,007 (28.6%)

The Governor believed he was going to lose, but he did not imagine that his defeat would be nearly as great as it was. Catts carried only the counties of Holmes, Okaloosa, and Washington. All three of the counties were in rural west Florida where Cattsism was the strongest.

Florida's establishment Democrats were ecstatic at the defeat of Cattsism and the defeat of every candidate supported by the Catts organization. One paper opined that the primary emphasized "the determination to be rid of the whole thing." The paper continued that "Four years of Cattsism with its appealing prejudices, its personal aggrandizement, its selfishly hoping to withstand attack by pledging to organized labor, has showed Florida what might be, what would be if the people did not wake up and exert themselves." Another paper stated, "Florida has had her lesson that the pulpit is a failure in politics."

However, many of those that favored Catts held that the defeat of Cattsism was a result of other candidates deserting the Governor. The *Palm Beach Post* lamented, "Some men who were old-line Catts men, including Van Swearingen [a candidate for Governor in 1920], attempted to get away from Sidney J. Catts and in doing so got what they deserved - DEFEAT."

While the 1920 primary did repudiate Catts, it did not indicate that the repudiation was due mainly to his extreme bigotry. Catts was in many ways a man ahead of his times. He was much more progressive in some areas than most Floridians, especially the courthouse ring that controlled the Democratic Party. Catts faithfully supported prison reform, equality for women, expanded government services, labor rights, prohibition, and better education. Those controlling the Democratic Party had no particular affection for any of those positions in 1920.

25. *No More Victories*

SIDNEY J. Catts had suffered a disastrous defeat, but he didn't consider his political career over. He deluded himself into believing that he could rebuild his machine before he left office, and that he could use that machine to resurrect his political career later. He told himself, without justification, that in 1924, he could again make his case before the people and they would elect him Governor again.

Catts tasked James Hodges, Jerry Carter, and Joe Earman to hold what was left of his crumbling coalition together and to begin to rebuild it. What Catts did not understand was that without the power of incumbency he could not use patronage as a hammer to refashion his machine. Beyond that, Catts still could not contain his volatile personality and he soon destroyed what little of his organization that remained.

The last gasp of Cattsism came in December 1920, when Catts and Earman had a loud, ugly argument over the appointment of Edgar C. Thompson as the new State's Attorney for West Palm Beach. Earman did not think Thompson was the best choice for the job and he opposed the appointment. Earman was certain that he had convinced the Governor to choose someone else for State's Attorney. However, Catts eventually ignored the opinion of his advisor and appointed Thompson anyway.

Fed up with the outgoing Governor, Earman wrote a scalding editorial in which he said that the Governor tended to agree with the last person that spoke to him, that Catts would not keep his word, and that the Governor lacked "consistency and "fidelity." A distraught Earman wrote, "I believed in him [but] at the finish, he has disappointed me."

When he learned of the editorial, Catts exploded, say to Earman, "If you publish one more page in your paper like this last one . . . I will go to West Palm Beach with my double-barrel shotgun loaded with buckshot and have a final settlement with you."

Hodges tried to manufacture some type of reconciliation between Catts an Earman, but it was impossible. With the death of his friendship with Earman, so died the Catts political machine.

Despite the fact that Catts had nothing left but the remnants of his Cracker Army, he ran for Democratic nomination for Governor in both 1924 and 1928. It remains amazing that he was able to retain about the same percentage of votes in those two primaries as he received in 1920. Catts received 28.6% of the vote in 1924 and 27.1% in 1928.

In the 1928 contest, Catts came close to winning the primary in a crowded field. Catts had a strong issue in that his last bid for the Governor's chair. Catts ran against eventual Democratic presidential nominee, Alfred E. Smith. Smith was a Catholic and Catts dusted off his anti-Catholic rhetoric and nearly pulled an upset in the primary.

One problem for Catts in his latter campaigns was that he had a record. He spent most of his time on the defensive answering questions about his Administration, and could not gain traction with any new issues. For instance, in 1928, he found himself having to answer several charges against him. He also had to answer new charges made against him.

At one campaign stop in 1928, Catts, his voice not nearly as strong as it had been twelve years earlier said, "Some of my friends are asking that I explain what I meant in my speech referring to the Bootleggers' vote. I meant this – The Bootlegger and his friends' votes are large enough to elect a candidate to any office in Florida. This vote includes the Bootlegger and his customers of every walk of life. If there is a candidate who does not want this vote let him say so.

"I wish to announce also that there is not any truth in the rumors that my campaign is being financed by any Secret Order, Church, Ku-Klux-Klan, Al Smith or Gasoline Tax Money.

"As to my pardoning men convicted of criminal assault, no prisoners of this class have ever been pardoned in the history of Florida. All pardons can only be granted by an affirmative vote of the Board of Pardons, consisting of five members, the Governor having only one vote."

Then, Catts finally got to promises he had wanted to talk about in the beginning. He said he would give Floridians "more and bigger farms, ship building plants and factories with plenty of work for the working men . . ."

After the 1928 election, Catts never sought another political office.

26. Later Life

AFTER his term ended, Catts returned to his farm near DeFuniak Springs, but he didn't have his heart into farming. His citrus growing business quickly proved unsuccessful.

Catts was better at selling and he opened a real estate office, but the business failed too.

Later, Catts went into quackery and sold patent medicines. He marketed mostly alcohol-filled drinks with no medicinal properties such as *Catts' Hog Tonic*. However, that endeavor failed as well.

The year after his last attempt to win the Governor's office, authorities arrested Catts and he stood trial for counterfeiting, but a jury acquitted him.

Catts remained energetic even as he grew older. He spent several hours each day in his garden. Then he came inside, flopped down on his couch, and read. Catts was a vociferous reader and he could read for eight to ten hours continuously without a break.

Catts died at DeFuniak Springs March 9, 1936 at the age of seventy-two. His family buried his remains in the Magnolia Cemetery. There was little public notice given to his passing.

Conclusion

SIDNEY Johnston Catts was perhaps the most colorful and controversial politician ever to be elected Governor of Florida. He was able to win election even though he didn't have much money, and his chosen party didn't support him. He prevailed in politics by making himself the champion of the poor and the disaffected.

In addition, no matter what else one may say of Sidney Johnston Catts, he was a natural-born leader. In addition, while one can attest to the wrongness of some of his views, no one can doubt his fearlessness in advocating those views.

While no one should embrace the bigotry Catts preached, one should remember that he was a product of his time. His views were current and popular in the early 20th Century and even the President of the United States, Woodrow Wilson, shared them in large part.

It is unfortunate that he ill rewarded the Prohibition Party that gave him his second chance when his Democratic nomination was stolen from him. Even so, the election of Sidney J. Catts as Governor of Florida in 1916 illustrates that a vigorous candidate can win an election, with the right timing, and under the proper circumstances, despite an 'unpopular' party banner.

Never a Prohibition Party man, Catts reverted to the Democratic Party immediately after his election as Governor and did much to revitalize it by opening it to participation by many younger people.

In sum, Sidney Johnston Catts was a complex man living in a complex time and he deserves both praise and condemnation.

Appendix I:
Inaugural Address of Sidney J. Catts

*B*ELOW is the complete inaugural address delivered by Governor Catts:

"Citizens of Florida: This is the supreme hour of your triumph, to have gained this victory over all the forces of opposition so masterful and strong as were those that stood arrayed against you; and to have withstood them and conquered them, places this hour of your success with the historic ones, when the people of England raised Cromwell to peer, or when the citizens of France desolated the feudal system in the rejection of the Catholic hierarchy, and the kingcraft of that age, by the French Revolution, or when the colonies of America stood by Thomas Jefferson as he gave the world the supremest bill of man's rights, the Declaration of Independence.

"Your triumph is no less in this good hour in beautiful Florida, for you have withstood the onslaughts of the county and state political rings, the vast corporations, and the railroads, the fierce opposition of the daily and weekly press, and the organization of the Negro voters of the state against you, the judiciary of state partisan to your needs, and the power of the Roman Catholic hierarchy against you. Yet, over all these the common people of Florida, the everyday masses of the cracker people have triumphed, and the day of your apotheosis has arrived, and you can say, as said the ancient Hebrew devotee, 'Lift up your gates, and be ye lifted up, ye everlasting doors, and let the Lord of Glory in. Who is this Lord of Glory? The Lord of Hosts, He is the King of Glory.'

"In my days of fervid youthful imagination I have often wondered what could be the crowning achievement of a human ambition, and have pictured some things which might satiate human power, or crown ambition's desire. I have imagined that to be a great Rothschild of finance and hold the riches of a hemisphere in my hands, or to be a Morgan and listen to the monetary praise of the Americas, while the crowned heads and potentates of the Old World bowed to my financial requests, would be the meed of human endeavor, or the goal of man's distinction. I have dreamed to be a great preacher like John the Baptist, Christmas Evans, John Knox, and Charles Wesley, or the superb Talmadge, and sway the masses of mankind to repentance and to tears before Christ, and the throne of the supernal, would be the supremest achievement of the race, and the crowning event of man's lofty ambitions. I have sometimes thought that to be a great traveler and stand on Sahara's scorching borders or amid the arctic's polar snows and hear the gaunt wolf far-flung on Alaska's barren shore, or stand on ship deck beneath the equator's lurid touch and gauge at night upon the splendor of the Southern Cross, or rest at noonday upon the lofty height of the Andes or the snow crowned peaks of the Himalayas, or

'Sail upon the Rhine and Rhone
And view Mount Aetna's fiery side,
And see the Italian sunset sky,
Blend with the Adriatic Sea,
And hear the shout of fisherman
Along the shores of Galilee.'

could crown every ambition as a noted traveler and satisfy the desires of the soul.

"I have thought that to be a great warrior, and like Alexander, Caesar, Anthony, Cromwell, Napoleon, Washington, Grant or Lee, lead the charging squadrons of earth to noble battle for the right, and read one's history in a people's praise and gratitude, would be the lordliest of human anticipations. But my ideal has changes, and I stand to tell you, comrades and fellow citizens, that to triumph with my people in an hour like this is grander, far, than all else to me. To be under God and my noble constituents an apostle of a new nation-sweeping tenet and political doctrine, which doctrine is 'nothing in Florida above the nation's flag.' The little red schoolhouse to stand as an emblem of the nation's liberty. No money to be given for any sectarian schools from our treasury forever; the freedom of speech, conscience, and press, and entire separation of church and state forever; to vote for no man for any office, nor appoint any, who owes his allegiance to a foreign national potentate, or foreign ecclesiastical power on American soil; the suppression of the whiskey traffic for state and nation, and the crowing political dogma for all, 'America for Americans throughout eternity.' Here is to my mind all the greatness that any should crave, and you, my comrades, have given to me this victory today, and in it I am supremely happy and blessed. With my hat off, and as Jacob of old, facing Bethel, I stand in mute and silent gratitude to you and God, my fellow citizens and comrades and thank you for this glad hour, the hour of your political triumph and power.

"I had rather stand here today as your apostle of victory and success in these great political doctrines than to live in any other age of the world's great history. If only the God of our fathers will give me the grace, wisdom and judgment to serve you and Him, and make you the governor I desire to be, and like Solomon of old, I lift my voice to the Supreme Architect of the universe today for these great gifts that I so much desire and need, and as he said, so said I, 'Master I am only a little child before Thee, I know not how to rule this great people, which is like the dust of the earth in number. Give me, O Lord God, I pray Thee, wisdom and knowledge, that I may judge this Thy people and rule them aright.'

"Citizens of my beloved and adopted state, there are many problems to confront us in the next four years, and with your help and confidence, and with the mutual respect and consideration for each other by the Legislature, the Senate, and the Chief Executive, we hope to master many of these perplexing problems.

"The most important thing facing Florida today is the drainage of the Everglades, and if the incoming administration can succeed in doing this in the next four years, an event of as much moment will have transpired in the history of Florida as the opening of the Panama Canal was to the world. The first step in this direction, as I see it, would be an awakening of the people of Florida to the greatness of the project. I have recently returned from a trip through the Everglades and Lake Okeechobee, which showed me the immense richness of the section to be drained. To my mind, this is now the richest section on earth today, and so rich is the land, and so fertile its quality, that the land itself might be taken up and shipped just as it is as a fertilizer to the poorer sections of the state and the Union. This rich, black muck land runs six to eight feet deep throughout nearly the extent of the millions of acres, and produces the greatest crops I have seen anywhere in all my travels. One trouble about the matter is, the people living in other sections of the state are not in sympathy with the drainage of the Everglades as they should be. This we desire to develop by a speaking tour throughout the state at no distant future, so that a spirit of cooperation and enlistment may be awakened everywhere. The first great project after this will be the floating of the first (about) $3,000,000 worth of bonds, and after that $3,000,000 more, which should put the whole section largely in a condition of cultivation, and after the first crop is made on this land you may look for prices to soar until the fabulous prices of California will be nothing to what this, the richest land on earth will bring. I guess I had better before you call me a prophet.

The next thing that will claim our attention will be the cutting out of all waste in the administration of state institutions and industries. It is an established fact that when the same officials continue too long at their jobs, that they let in extravagances here and there, until by and by great methods of waste are established, and the state loses many thousands of dollars per year because of lack of system upon the part of those whose business it is to see after her affairs. Our idea will be to effect changes in these matters by rotation in office and putting in new men as far as we can do so practically; and in case these men do not make good, put them out and put others in until we find the right men.

"The next thing that will claim our attention will be giving the Board of Equalization of Taxes more power, so that they shall not only have the right to equalize large and vast estates of private persons and corporations, but their privileges shall be extended to the vast systems of railways now penetrating our state. We notice that they have already effected great good in St. Johns County in the matter of the Flagler estate, whose taxes they raised from $75,000 to $16,000,000, which increased the taxes of St. Johns County $107,000, state and county, and decreased the millage from ten mills to five. This will pay their salaries for many years and shows what they could do were the adequately equipped with legal authority and had the right kind of men on the board. It will be our pleasure to try to get the legislature to see that this body should be given full and competent power to equalize the taxes of all property lying within our domain.

"The primary law will also come in for its change, as the recent election muddle proved conclusively that it is very deficient in regard to second choice votes. Just what the changes are to be cannot yet be said, but we notice that many newspapers of the state are taking this matter up, and are insisting upon it that the law shall be simplified and the second choice vote cut out entirely. Our suggestion will be that not only this change be wrought, but that others also be effected which will materially change conditions of collusion and fraud, and which will simplify the ballot to an extent that 'the wayfaring man, though a fool, need not err therein.'

Many of our sober and best thinking men also think that the time has come in the history of our state when the initiative, referendum and recall laws shall be put upon our statute books and become a corporate part of the laws of the land. They also think that, with proper provisions of protection, these laws should run the gauntlet from constable to the highest officers of the state, and thus insure in times of danger that no czar-like procedure shall ever be taken part in by any official or set of officials.

"Another problem that will come up for solution upon the initiative of the House and Senate, will be the matter of Prohibition. This is a question which, like Banquo's ghost, will not down until it shall be finally settled for what is best to the greater masses of mankind. The whiskey men of the state all feel that it is a question which will ultimately go against them, not only in Florida, but in the nation.

The next question that will come before us for solution will be the opening of all closed institutions within the state of Florida for police inspections, such as convents, parochial schools and other institutions of like nature. The taxing of all church property, with the exception of the pastoral homes and the churches themselves, and the same universal examinations for all teachers, whether they be in public or parochial or denominational schools. This possibly will have some disquieting effects upon legislation, but like the great question of Prohibition will never be down until it is settled upon a basis of Americanism.

Another question which will claim the best thought and attention of our House and Senate is the matter of industrial schools and training for the boys and girls of Florida. As Senator Williams says, the time is past when boys and girls Know all about Latin, Greek, French, Hebrew, Sanskrit and all the dead languages and yet when they go to sell goods right, or retain their positions, and when they go to farm 'it will take two years to make their sugarcane grow big enough to chew.' If we desire to retain the respect of ourselves and the nations of the earth, we must educate the hand as well as the brain. This is one of the great schemes which we hope to see instituted in Florida in the next four years.

"Another question of vital importance will be to get cooperation between the people and the railroads of the state, by a system of properly regulated freight rates which will insure to them the early shipment of their commodities, vegetables and fruit, no discrimination against them and such thorough cooperation as shall put the magnificent productions of Florida into on the same basis of railroad cooperation as California now enjoys. To do this we must have the attention of the railroads to such an extent that they must attend to the wants of Florida with no less avidity, by having plenty of cars always on hand, rapid transportation, low freight rates etc., as now marks the shipping facilities from the wheat and corn regions of the West and from the fruit regions of California. Such conditions as these will make Florida the golden state of the nation.

"Standing as we do today, without the pale of specific knowledge, it is impossible for us to tell of many evils that should be corrected Suffice it to say that with the help and cooperation of all the forces involved in these matters, we shall strive as best we can to correct each and every one of them as they may present themselves. One cannot but feel how helpless he is until faced with such grave responsibilities as will confront him as the Chief Executive of the state, and in such an hour as this we feel that we may say with the consecrated poet of old, with his faith fixed in the Almighty and his fellow creatures:

"'I know not where his islands lift
Their fronded palms in air;
I only know we cannot drift
Beyond his love and care.
I know not what the future hath
Of marvel or surprise,
Assured alone that life and death
His mercy underlies.'

"This age of ours is marked by a revival of patriotism upon the part of the state and the nation. In most of the southern states, conditions have grown into the same mould as in the antebellum day, with the exception of slavery. Therefore society in its crudeness is fixed and firmly established in grooves which cannot be changed or molested. In Florida, conditions are very dissimilar on account of the cosmopolitan nature of our population. Here the New World and the Old grapple for power. Here the Old South, with its settled habits of society, is thrown together with the restless forces of the East, while the miner from Arizona or Alaska comes in contact with the Cuban, Spaniard, or inhabitant of the Old World. This condition of mingled society; forced of habit, trend of thought, and variation of citizenship, has not reached its fruition, nor has the settled character of inhabitants and citizenship yet been wrought. This is necessarily bound to cause much thought on the part of us all, and while we look at our allegiance to our state from many angles, we can say, with Tallahassee's splendid young Poet Laureate Professor Benjamin Benson Lane,

> "'Florida thy matchless state,
> Of all thy sons the ready toast,
> Around thy thousand miles of coast
> The South Seas toss, and toss and wait
> The day, when from harbor-bar and strait,
> Shall sally forth the nation's fleets,
> And Make thy gulf a sea of streets,
> That lead all to Pacific's gate.
> 'Tis here that Fate and Purpose meets,
> That Chance and Will may harmonize;
> Today the tale of time completes;
> Hither the world shall turn its eyes,
> North East and West shall mingle here;
> Arouse thy sons – their day draws near!

> "'Their day draws near! Arouse them then;
> Give them the mastery of the wealth,
> A climate rate, exuding health,
> A perfect land beyond men's ken.
> Let not the welcomed stranger, when
> He cometh find himself more fit,
> Nor better trained his native wit;
> This is the land to grow true men.
> Floridians all, this land is ours,
> And we that love it love to serve.
> God strengthen every heart and nerve
> Whene'er a danger near us lowers.
> Alert, courageous, ready – all
> Answer the throbbing future's call.'

"In conclusion, there is but one thought further that I desire to bring to your notice. Our state I so rich in all that makes for material wealth as a people we may be prone to forget the benign hand of Him who has given it all to us. When we contemplate the millions of forest lands, teeming with turpentine, rosin and lumber; our lakes, estuaries, bays, gulfs and rivers thronging with fish, and the crustaceans of every tribe; the splendid muck lands of the everglades; the acres of yellow gem citrus fruits; the millions of sheep, hogs and cattle; the rolling prairies of the southern peninsula; the thriving villages, hamlets, towns and cities; the soaring prices of our land, the magnificent climate, and the teeming trains bearing their hundreds of thousands to the state, we as a people are prone to forget that the one aim of life is, not to acquire knowledge or obtain wealth, but that there is a higher, a grander, a nobler principle of living, and that is the same thought expressed in Kipling's great 'Recessional,' when the people, drunk with the tumult of England's mighty glory in the jubilee of their splendid queen, caused him to repeat with prayerful consideration this wonderful hymn, bringing the people back to a knowledge of God and the consciousness of the fact that it was His hand that had given them all this wonderful glory, and with this poem, as a prayer to our ever-to-be-adorned and conquering God, we will close:

"'God of our fathers, known of old –
Lord of our far-flung battle line –
Beneath whose awful hand we hold

Dominion over palm and pine –
Lord God of Hosts, be with us yet,
Lest we forget – lest we forget!

"'The tumult and the shouting dies –
The captains and the kings depart –
Still stands Thine ancient sacrifice,
An humble and contrite heart.
Lord God of Hosts, be with us yet,
Lest we forget – lest we forget!

"'Far –called, our navies melt away –
On dune and headland sinks the fire –
Lo, all our pomp of yesterday,
Is one with Nineveh and Tyre,
Judge of the Nations, spare us yet,
Lest we forget – lest we forget!

"'If, drunk with sight of power, we loose
Wild tongues that have not Thee in awe –
Such boasting as the Gentiles use,
Or lesser breeds without the Law –
Lord God of Hosts, be with us yet,
Lest we forget – lest we forget!

"'For heathen heart that put her trust
In reeking tube and iron sword –
All valiant dust that builds on dust,
And guarding, calls not Thee to guard –
For frantic boast and foolish word,
Thy mercy on thy People, Lord!'"

Appendix II:
1916 Prohibition Party National Platform

THE Prohibition Party, assembled in its Twelfth National Convention in the city of St. Paul, Minnesota, on this Twentieth day of July, 1916, grateful to Almighty God for the blessings of liberty, for our institutions and the multiplying signs of early victory for the cause for which the Party stands in order that the people may know the source of its faith and the basis of its action, should it be clothed with governmental power, challenges the attention of the Nation and asks the votes of the people on this Declaration of principles.

We denounce the traffic in intoxicating liquors. We believe in its abolition. It is a crime — not a business — and should not have governmental sanction.

We demand — and if given power, we will effectuate the demand — that the manufacture, importation, exportation, transportation and sale of alcoholic beverage purposes shall be prohibited.

To the accomplishment of that end, we pledge the exercise of all governmental power and amendment of statutes and the amendment of constitutions, State and National. Only by a political party committed to this purpose can such policy be made effective. We call upon all voters, so believing, to place the Prohibition Party in power upon this issue as a necessary step in the solution of the liquor problem.

The right of citizens of the United States to vote should not be denied or abridged by the United States or by any State on account of sex. We declare in favor of the enfranchisement of women by amendments to State and Federal Constitutions.

We condemn the Republican and Democratic parties for their failure to submit an equal suffrage amendment to the National Constitution. We remind the four million women voters that our Party was the first to declare for their political rights, which it did in 1872. We invite their co-operation in electing the Prohibition Party to power.

We are committed to the policy of peace and friendliness with all nations. We are unalterably opposed to the wasteful military programme of the Democratic and Republican parties. Militarism protects no worthy institution. It endangers them all. It violates the high principles which have brought us as a Nation to the present hour. We are for a constructive programme in preparedness for peace. We declare for and will promote a world court, to which national differences shall be submitted, so maintained as to give its decrees binding force.

We will support a compact among nations to dismantle navies and disband armies, but until such court and compact are established we pledge ourselves to maintain an effective army and navy and to provide coast defenses entirely adequate for national protection.

We are opposed to universal military service, and to participation in the rivalry that has brought Europe to the shambles and now imperils the civilization of the race.

Private profit, so far as constitutionally possible, should be taken out of the manufacture of war munitions and all war equipment.

In normal times we favor the employment of the army in vast reclamation plans, in reforesting hills and mountains, in building State and National highways, in the construction of an inland waterway from Florida to Maine, in the opening of Alaska and in unnumbered other projects which will make our soldiers constructive builders of peace. For such service there should be paid an adequate individual wage.

Those units of our navy which are capable of being converted into merchantmen and passenger vessels should be constructed with that purpose in view, and chiefly so utilized in times of peace.

We condemn the political parties, which for more than thirty years have allowed munition and war equipment manufacturers to plunder the people and to jeopardize the highest interest of the Nation by furnishing honeycombed armour plate and second rate battleships which the Navy League now declares are wholly inadequate.

We will not allow the country to forget that the first step toward physical, economic, moral and political preparedness is the enactment of National Prohibition.

The countries at war are preparing for a fierce industrial struggle to follow the cessation of hostilities. As a matter of commercial economy, international friendliness, business efficiency, and as a help to peace, we demand that reciprocal trade treaties be negotiated with all nations with which we have trade relations. A commission of specialists, free from the control of any party, should be appointed with power to gather full information of all phases of the questions of tariff and reciprocity, and to recommend such legislation as it deems necessary for the welfare of American business and labor.

The necessity of legislation to enable American ship builders or owners to meet foreign competition, on the most favorable terms, is obvious.

Materials for construction should be admitted free of duty.

The purchase of ships abroad, when low prices invite, should be allowed and, when so purchased, should be admitted to American registry.

Harbor rules and charges and navigation laws should not be onerous, but favorable to the highest degree.

Liberal payment should be made by the Government for the carrying of mails or for transport services.

All shipping from the United States to any of our possessions should be reserved to ships of American registry.

The people should not overlook the fact that the effect of Nationwide Prohibition, on labor and industry generally, will be such as to lower the cost of ship building per unit, and at the same time permit the payment of higher wages. The increased volume of trade and commerce, which will result, when the wastage of the liquor traffic is stopped, will quicken our shipping on every sea and send our flag on peaceful missions into every port. This is urged as an incidental effect of wise action on the liquor question, but is none the less to be desired and will aid in the solution of the problem of our merchant marine.

Mexico needs not a conqueror, but a good Samaritan. We are opposed to the violation of the sovereignty of the Mexican people, and will countenance no war of aggression against them. We pledge the help of this country in the suppression of lawless bands of marauders and murderers, who have taken the lives of American citizens, on both sides of the border, as well as of Mexicans in their own country.

The lives and property of our citizens, when about their lawful pursuits, either in the United States or in Mexico, must and will be protected. In the event of a break-down of government across the border, we would use, in the interests of civilization, the force necessary for the establishment of law and order.

In this connection we affirm our faith in the Monroe Doctrine, proclaimed in the early days of the Nation's life and unswervingly maintained for nearly a hundred years.

We cannot claim the benefits of the Doctrine and refuse to assume or discharge the responsibility and the duties which inhere therein and flow therefrom. Those duties have long been unmet in Mexico. We should meet them now, acting, not for territory, not for conquest or for ourselves alone, but for and with all the nations of North and South America.

The Democratic party has blundered, and four years ago the Republican party evaded and passed on the problem it now asks the opportunity to solve. The abandonment of the Philippines at this time would be an injustice to them and a violation of our plain duty. As soon as they are prepared for self-government, by education and training, they should be granted their independence on terms just to themselves and us.

We reaffirm our declaration in favor of conservation of forests, water power and other natural resources.

Departmental decisions ought not to be final, but the rights of the people should be protected by provision for court review.

In order that the public service may be of the highest standard, the government should be a model employer in all respects. To enforce the civil service law in spirit as well as in letter, all promotions should be nonpolitical, based only upon proven fitness; all recommendations for demotions or removals from the service should be subjected to the review of a nonpartisan board or commission.

The merit system should be extended to cover all postmasters, collectors of revenue, marshals and other such public officials whose duties are purely administrative.

We reaffirm our allegiance to the principle of secure tenure of office, during good behavior and capable effort, as the means of obtaining expert service. We declare for the enactment of an equitable retirement law for disabled and super-annuated employees, in return for faithful service rendered, to maintain a high degree of efficiency in public office.

We stand for Americanism. We believe this country was created for a great mission among the nations of the earth. We rejoice in the fact that it has offered asylum to the oppressed of other lands and for those, more fortunately situated, who yet wished to improve their condition. It is the land of all peoples and belongs not to any one—it is the heritage of all. It should come first in the affections of every citizen, and he who loves another land more than this is not fit for citizenship here, but he is a better citizen who, loving his country, has reverence for the land of his fathers and gains from its history and traditions that which inspires him to nobler service to the one in which he lives.

The Federal Government should interest itself in helping the newcomer into that vocation and locality where he shall most quickly become an American. Those fitted by experience and training for agricultural pursuits should be encouraged to develop the millions of acres of rich and idle land.

We favor uniform marriage and divorce laws, the extermination of polygamy and the complete suppression of the traffic in women and girls. Differences between capital and labor should be settled through arbitration, by which the rights of the public are conserved as well as those of the disputants. We declare for the prohibition of child labor in factories, mines and workshops; an eight hour maximum day, with one day of rest in seven; for more rigid sanitary requirements and such working conditions as shall foster the physical and moral well-being of the unborn; for the protection of all who toil, by the extension of Employers' Liability Acts; for the adoption of safety appliances for the safeguarding of labor; and for laws that will promote the just division of the wealth which labor and capital jointly produce. Provision should be made for those who suffer from industrial accidents and occupational diseases.

We pledge a business-like administration of the Nation's affairs; the abolition of useless offices, bureaus and commissions; economy in the expenditure of public funds; efficiency in governmental service; and the adoption of the budget system. The president should have power to veto any single item or items of an appropriation bill.

We condemn, and agree when in power to remedy, that which is known as 'pork barrel' legislation, by which millions of dollars have been appropriated for rivers where there is no commerce, harbors where there are no ships and public buildings where there is no need.

We are in favor of a single presidential term of six years.

Public utilities and other resources that are natural monopolies are at the present time exploited for personal gain under a monopolistic system. We demand the public ownership or control of all such utilities by the people and their operation and administration in the interests of all the people. We stand for the preservation and development of our free institutions and for absolute separation of church and state with the guaranty of full religious and civil liberty.

We stand for the rights, safety, justice and development of humanity; we believe in the equality of all before the law; in old-age pensions and insurance against unemployment and in help for needy mothers, all of which could be provided from what is now wasted for drink.

We favor the initiative, referendum and recall.

While it is admitted that grain and cotton are fundamental factors in our national life, it cannot be denied that proper assistance and protection are not given these commodities at terminal markets, in the course of inter-state commerce.

We favor and pledge our efforts to obtain grain elevators at necessary terminal markets, such elevators to be owned and operated by the Federal Government; also to secure Federal grain inspection under a system of civil service and to secure the abolition of any Board of Trade, Chamber of Commerce, or other place of gambling in grain or trading in `options' or 'futures' or 'short-selling,' or any other form of so-called speculation wherein products are not received or delivered, but wherein so-called contracts are settled by the payment of 'margins' or 'differences' through clearing houses or otherwise.

This Party stands committed to free and open markets based upon legitimate supply and demand, absolutely free from questionable practices or market manipulation. We also favor government warehouses for cotton at proper terminals where the interests of producers require the same; and the absolute divorce of all railroad elevators or warehouses owned by railroad companies, either public or private, from operation and control of private individuals in competition with the public in merchandising grain, cotton or other farm products.

We furthermore endorse all proper methods among producers of those means of co-operative mutual enterprise, which tend toward broader and better markets for both producer and consumer.

This is the day of opportunity for the American people. The triumph of neither old political party is essential to our safety or progress. The defeat of either will be no public misfortune. They are one party. By age and wealth, by membership and traditions, by platforms and in the character of their candidates, they are the Conservative Party of the United States. The Prohibition Party as the promoter of every important measure of social justice presented to the American people in the last two generations, and as the originator of nearly all such legislation, remains now the only great Progressive Party.

The patriotic voters, who compose the Republican and Democratic parties, can, by voting the Prohibition ticket this year, elect the issue of National Prohibition.

To those, in whatever party, who have the vision of a land redeemed from drink, we extend a cordial invitation to join with us in carrying the banner of Prohibition to Nationwide victory.

Appendix III:
Florida Election Returns from 1916

*B*ELOW are election returns from Florida in 1916:

Florida gubernatorial election:
Sidney J. Catts (Proh.): 39,546 (47.71%)
William V. Knott (Dem.): 30,343 (36.61%)
George W. Allen (Rep.): 10,333 (12.47%)
C. C. Allen (Soc.): 2,470 (2.9%)
Others: 193 (0.2%)

Presidential vote in Florida:
Woodrow Wilson (Dem.): 55,984 (69.34%)
Charles E. Hughes (Rep.): 14,611 (18.1%)
Allan Benson (Soc.): 5,353 (6.63%)
James Hanly (Proh.) 4,786 (5.93%)

Selected Sources

"As Viewed From Cuba". *Punta Gorda Herald*, Punta Gorda, Florida, October 12, 1916.

Bond, Bill. "Rape Case Put County In Midst Of Controversy", *Orlando Sentinel*, September 10, 1986

Burns, Frank. "Cumberland University Law School", *Tennessee Encyclopedia*. Nashville: Tennessee Historical Society, October 8, 2017.

"Catts Addresses Voters." Montgomery Advertiser, October 29, 1904.

Clark, James C. (Edited by Rowland Stiteler) "What Was The Catts Scam?" *Orlando Sentinel*, January 11, 1987

Clark, James C. "Anti-catholic Bigotry Almost Became Law", *Orlando Sentinel*, May 22, 1994.

Clark, James C. "Past Inaugurals Have Been Time For Dirty Deals", *Orlando Sentinel*, January 6, 1991

Clark, James C. "The Year 1916 Was A Strange One For Electing A Governor" *Orlando Sentinel*, February 7, 1993.

Clark, Jim. "Anti-catholic Fervor Led To Violence In Gainesville", *Orlando Sentinel*, March 15, 1998

Clarkson, Brent, "Remember the 1916 Florida recount? Neither do we, but it might have been more contentious than this one", *South Florida Sun Sentinel*, November 16, 2018

Colby, Frank M., editor. *The New International Year Book*. New York: Dodd, Mead and Company, 1917.

Flynt, Wayne. *Cracker Messiah: Governor Sidney J. Catts of Florida*. Baton Rouge, Louisiana: Louisiana State University, 1977.

Gaustad, Edwin Scott, and Phillip L. Barrow. *New Historical Atlas of Religion in America 3rd Edition*. Oxford: Oxford University Press, 2001.

Jennings, Warren A. "Sidney J. Catts and the Democratic Primary of 1920." *Florida Historical Society Quarterly, Vol. 39, Issue 3*, July, 1960.

Kerber, Stephen. "Park Trammell and the Florida Democratic Senatorial Primary of 1916". *Florida Historical Quarterly*, January 1980.

Kleindienst, Linda. "Florida Inaugurals: From Solemn To Silly", *Fort Lauderdale News*, January 7, 1987.

Lord, Dorothy. *Sidney J. Catts and the Gubernatorial Election of 1916*. Apalachicola, Florida: Apalachee Publishing, 1963-1967.

McIlver, Stuart. "The Gunslinging Governor." *South Florida Sun Sentinel*, September 29, 1996.

"Mr. Catts Announces." *Montgomery Advertiser*, March 4, 1904."

Mormino, Gary R., "Perspective: The man who switched, then won." *Tampa Bay Times*, October 10, 2014.

Porter, Kirk H. and Donald Bruce Johnson, editors. *National Party Platforms 1840-1968*. Champaign: University of Illinois Press, 1972.

Powers, Ormund. "Pistol-packing Race For Governor Was An Upset In Several Ways." *Orlando Sentinel*, November 3, 1999.

Proctor, Samuel, editor. *The Florida Historical Quarterly*. Florida Historical Society, October 1970.

Robinson, Jim. "Florida Wasn't Wet And Wild, For A Time", *Orlando Sentinel*, May 7, 1995

Robison, Jim. "Bag Of Dirty Tricks Helped Florida Elect A Governor", *Orlando Sentinel*, November 14, 1999.

Schaal, Peter. *Sanford as I Knew It, 1912-1935*. Self-published, 1970.

"Sidney J. Catts Assumes Governorship of Florida While Thousands Cheer". *The Pensacola Journal*. Pensacola, Florida, January 3, 1917.

Stiteler, Rowland. "Trivia File" *Orlando Sentinel*, September 28, 1986

Storms, Roger C. *Partisan Prophets: A History of the Prohibition Party*. Denver, Colorado: National Prohibition Foundation, 1972.

"Sturkie For Catts". *Tampa Tribune*, July 21, 1916.

Thornton, J. Mills. "Alabama Politics, J. Thomas Heflin, and the Expulsion Movement in 1929." *Alabama Review 21*, April 1968.

Ward, Sarah F. *The White Ribbon Story: 125 Years of Service to Humanity*. Evansville, Illinois: Signal Press, 1999.

About the Author

CL Gammon has had a life-long fascination with American History and with the written word. These joint fascinations have led to his becoming an award winning and an internationally known bestselling author of more than fifty books. Gammon, who studied Political Science at Tennessee Technological University and History and Government at Hillsdale College, has entertained and educated readers for two decades. Several universities, including the State University of New York and the University of Akron and others, have used his books as course material. In addition, articles written by Gammon have appeared in more than a dozen national and regional publications. Gammon also writes feature stories for his hometown newspaper, the *Macon County Times*. Gammon is the CEO of Deep Read Press. Gammon lives in Lafayette, Tennessee.

Index

Abbey, St.Leo's: 41, 84

African Americans: 41, 45, 77, 80, 84-86, 112, 120, 124-126, 138

Alabama: (Dallas County: 11, 13-14, 16) (Fort Deposit: 17), (Lafayette: 21) (Lowndes County: 16, 24), (Mt. Willing: 16), (Pleasant Hill: 11, 17), (Sandy Ridge: 16), (Tuskegee: 17, 20, 24)

Alexander, James E.: 98, 101

Allen, C. C.: 72, 162

Allen, George W.: 58, 71-72, 162

American Civil Liberties Union (ACLU): 85-86

American Federation of Labor (A. F. L.): 123-125

Anti-Catholicism: 8, 1112, 16, 23-25, 33, 35-36, 38-46, 55-56, 58, 74, 80, 83-85, 89, 119-120, 128, 132, 138

Anti-foreignism: 8, 140-141, 154-155

Anti-Semitic: 35

Anti-Saloon League: 44

Auburn University: 13

Ball, Willis M.: 97

Baker, Purley: 44

Baltimore Sun: 123

Bank Guarantee Bill: 82, 99, 106

Bard, G. W.: 42

Barrs, John M.: 35

Benedict XV, Pope: 23, 40-41, 43, 51, 56, 58, 84

Bigotry: 8-9, 23, 28, 35, 41-42, 56, 83, 130, 136

Bilbo, Theodore: 8

Bingham, J. W.: 60-61

Blease, Cole: 8

Blitch, J. S.: 54, 90, 92, 104-105

Bloxham, William D: 31

Board of Control: 90, 94-96, 105

Bootleggers: 23, 137

Brett, H. J: 95

Bryan, Nathan P: 83

Bryan, William Jennings: 21

Bryan Primary Law: 49, 98

Bryan, William S.:31

Burke, J. V.: 54, 90

Camp Wheeler Affair: 120-122

Carolina, South: 8, 11

Carter, Jerry W.: 54, 90, 131

Catts, Adeline: 11

Catts, Alice May Campbell: 12

Catts' Hog Tonic: 135

Cattsism: 108, 115, 129, 131

Catts, Jacob: 11-12

Catts, Rozier: 85

Catts, Ruth: 92

Catts, Samuel W.: 11-12

Catts, Sidney, J.: (Acquitted of Murder: 25, 135), (Inauguration: 79-82, 138-150), (Insurance Agent: 19, 26, 48, 52), (Preacher: 15-19, 21-22, 26, 28, 45, 47, 54, 58, 60, 67, 139), (Student: 13-14)

Catts, Sidney J., Jr.: 92-93, 124

Central Powers: 83

Child Labor: 9, 63, 103, 119, 158

Christian, J. B.: 91, 111

Church: (Bethel Baptist: 17-18, 20), (DeFuniak First Baptist: 18-19), (Tuskegee First Baptist: 17)

Confederacy: 8, 11

Conservative: 8, 37, 65, 97, 113, 161

Conspiracy Theories: 36, 40, 44, 53, 67-68, 84

Corporations: 9, 33, 57, 80, 82, 89, 98, 103, 138, 143

Courthouse Ring: 26, 30, 38, 50-51, 60, 89, 96, 110, 130

Cox, W. H.: 54, 68, 91, 110-111

Cumberland University: 13-14, 70

D. C., Washington: 23, 42, 84, 110, 113, 115-116, 118, 121-123

DeFuniak Breeze: 69

Democratic Party: 9-10, 12, 20-21, 25-27, 30-32, 35-38, 40-41, 47, 50, 52-55, 57, 60, 62, 65, 67-72, 76-78, 80-81, 83, 87, 90-91, 96-97, 99, 101-102, 107-110, 112-113, 115, 122, 124, 127-130, 132, 136, 152, 156, 161-162

Earman, Joe: 79, 90, 95, 105, 131-132

Education: 9, 13-14, 33, 81, 90, 95-96, 98-99, 103-106, 130, 156

Europe: 24, 56, 83, 93, 153

Farmers' Union: 22, 115

Farris, Ion: 30, 32

Ferguson, James E.: 8

Fletcher, Duncan Upshaw: 31, 67, 109-110, 112-129

Florida: (Brevard County: 37, 119),

(Bronson: 126),
(Brooksville: 68),
(Chattahoochee: 31),
(Citrus County: 88),
(Clay County: 88),
(Columbia County: 97, 111), (Cracker: 28, 42, 44-45, 52, 54, 57, 68, 70, 72, 79-80, 110, 123, 128, 132, 139),
(DeFuniak Springs: 18-19, 54, 69, 95, 135),
(Deland: 98),
(Escambia County: 119),
(Gainesville: 42, 99),
(Gulf Coast: 28, 34),
(Hastings: 126),
(Hillsborough County: 37), (Holmes County: 129), (Jacksonville: 32, 35, 38, 54, 69, 83, 86, 91, 97, 113, 116, 124),
(Key West: 97), (Lake City: 54, 88), (Leesburg: 30-31), (Legislature: 30, 32-34, 49, 82, 89, 97-107, 123, 141, 144), (Live Oak: 116), (Madison: 118), (Miami: 32),
(Monroe County: 88, 101), (Okaloosa County: 129), (Palm Beach: 79, 90, 129, 131-132),
(Panhandle: 18, 28, 44, 52, 108), (Pasco County: 35, 85), (Pensacola: 18, 54, 70, 95, 119), (Polk County: 110), (Raiford: 90, 104-105, 118),
(Recount: 50-54, 56, 67, 69, 71), (State Executive Committee: 36-38, 54, 69, 77, 113), (State Federation of Labor: 37), (State Income Tax: 46), (St. Leo: 41), (St. Petersburg: 70, 127),
(Sumterville: 31),
(Supreme Court: 9, 14, 50, 54, 71, 80, 91 99),
(Tallahassee: 18, 33, 43, 47, 68, 89, 97, 116, 148),
(Tampa: 37-38, 41, 54, 69, 84, 91, 95),
(Wakulla Springs: 127),
(Washington County: 129), (Williams Park: 127), (Williston: 54),
(Winter Haven: 125)

Florida A & M: 95

Florida East Coast Railroad: 113

Florida St. College for Women: 94

Florida School for the Deaf & Blind: 94

Florida, University of

Flourney, W. W.: 93-95

Flynt, Wayne: 15

Ford, Model T: 43, 114

Foster, J. Clifford R.: 90-91

Frecker, C. T.: 92, 111

Friend of the Convict Office: 98

Gainesville Sun: 42, 99

Gambling: 65, 102, 160

Georgia: (Dawson: 31), (Fort McPherson: 93), (Macon: 17, 120)

Georgia Southern & Florida Railroad: 100

Germans: 24, 41, 56, 83-84
Gettysburg, Battle of: 11
Gilchrist, Albert W.: 31, 37
Gray, Robert Andrew: 47-48
Guardians of Liberty: 22, 35, 41-42
Gomez, Arthur: 97, 101
Gompers, Samuel: 123
Gordon, Anna Adams: 44
Guam Bill: 119
Guards, Macon: 17
Gulf Inland Waterways Association: 113
Hall, J. E.:
Hanly, James Frank: 67, 72, 162
Hardee, Cary A.: 117-118
Heflin, J. Thomas: 8, 21, 25
Herlong, Mark B.: 124
Hinshaw, Virgil G.: 61
Hodges, James B.: 54-55, 88-91, 95, 97, 99-100, 103, 131-132
Hodges, T. R.: 33-34, 88-89
Howard College: 13
Hudson, Frederick M.: 32, 69
Internal Revenue Service: 31
Italians: 86, 140

Florida Times-Union: 38, 69, 97, 104, 117
Jeffersonian, The: 35
Jefferson, Thomas: 87, 138
Jelks, William: 20
Jennings, Frank E.: 95
Johnson, James Weldon: 112
Knott, William V.: 27, 30-33, 37-38, 43, 4748, 50-53, 55, 58, 67-72, 162
Ku Klux Klan: 56
Lakeland Ledger: 70
League of Nations: 115, 118
Leper Colony: 122
Long, Huey: 8
Louisiana: 8
Lynching: 85-86, 91
McCants, James: 111
Mcclenny Standard: 122
Mack, W. Bryan: 54, 90, 95
Masonic Order: 21
Massachusetts, Boston: 24
Merchant Marine Act: 63, 116, 155
Mechanics, Junior Order of American: 21
Mexico: 63, 155-156
Mexico, Gulf of: 28, 34
Miles, Nelson: 42

171

Mississippi: 8
Mohr, Charles: 84
Murphree, A. A.: 95
NAACP: 85
Nativism: 28
Neal, Minnie E.: 44
Nepotism: 92-93, 96, 117
New York Times: 74
Raiford Prison: 90, 104-105, 118
Randall, Charles: 61
Republican Party: 72, 110, 126, 152, 156, 161-162
Roebuck, W. J.: 97, 101, 111-112
Paderick, K. R.: 92
Palm Beach Post, The: 79, 129
Patriotic Sons of America: 35
Parker, Billy: 39
Patriotism: 128, 147
Patronage: 87, 89, 96, 107, 117, 131
Pensacola Journal: 70
Pensacola News: 54
Phillips, W.W.: 111
Plympton, M. L.: 97
Poll Tax: 58-59
Populist: 8-9, 68
Priest: 58

Progressive: 9, 30, 32, 37, 46, 61, 65, 68, 79, 81, 130, 161
Protestant: 11, 23-24, 40-41, 45, 77, 84-85, 94
Prohibition: 9-10, 22-23, 44-45, 57, 60-67, 69, 72, 76, 81, 98, 101-12, 127, 130, 136, 144-145, 155-162
Pythias, Knights of: 22
Raney, George P.: 38
Reconstruction: 10-11, 16, 89, 126
Roamer: 34, 100
Roosevelt, Theodore: 68
Sanford Herald: 69
Sears Roebuck: 28, 57, 72
Sermon, Old Black Stump: 16
Smith, Alfred E.: 8
Smith, "Cotton" Ed: 132-133
Socialist Party: 68, 72, 162
Spoils System: 87, 96
St. Petersburg Times: 70
Straight-Out Democrats: 113
Sturkie Resolutions: 35-40, 54, 67
Sturkie, R. B.: 35-37, 51, 67

Suffrage, Woman's: 9, 46, 62, 82, 106, 152

Sutton, John B.: 95

Swearingen, Van C.: 54, 91, 129

Tampa Tribune: 69

Tennessee, Lebanon: 13

Thompson, Charles Winston: 20

Thompson, Edgar C.: 131

Tillman, Benjamin: 8

Trammell, Park: 26, 31, 37, 47, 83

Unions, Labor: 22, 82, 110, 115, 123

Vanderbilt University: 112

Vardaman, James K.: 8

Vicksburg, Battle of: 11

War, Civil: 8, 11-12, 32, 112

War, Revolutionary: 11

War, World: 24, 41, 56, 93, 120, 124, 126

Watson's Magazine: 35

Watson, Thomas E.: 8, 35

West, Thomas F.: 91

Wheeler, Wayne: 44

Wilhelm II, Kaiser: 41, 84

Wilson, Woodrow: 41, 63, 67, 72, 83-84, 114-115, 118, 136, 162

Woman's Christian Temperance Union (WCTU): 44-65, 61

Wood, Frank A.: 32

World, Woodmen of the: 21

Yonge, P. K.: 95

Young, William B.: 117

www.ingramcontent.com/pod-product-compliance
Lightning Source LLC
Chambersburg PA
CBHW071504040426
42444CB00008B/1488